DAILY BIBLE STUDY GUIDE

VOLUME II
THE NEW TESTAMENT

BY DR. DELRON SHIRLEY

2005
REVISED 2009

COVER DESIGN BY JEREMY SHIRLEY

To obtain permission to quote material from this book, please contact:

Delron Shirley
3210 Cathedral Spires Dr.
Colorado Springs, CO 80904
teachallnations@msn.com
www.teachallnationsmission.com

Week: One
Day: Monday
Book: Matthew
Chapter: One
Memory Verse: Twenty-three
Principle: The life principle of this chapter is that Jesus' birth was the prophetic fulfillment of God's promise to redeem fallen mankind.
Outline:

Verse 1 – Jesus is the son of Abraham and the son of David. These two Old Testament individuals characterized God's covenants with the people of Israel. Abraham had a covenant through his son which was to bless all the families of the earth. David had a covenant through his son that an heir would always rule in Jerusalem.

Verses 2-16 – Jesus' genealogy proves His lineage to the covenants of Abraham and David.

Verse 17 – All of God's redemptive history falls into segments of fourteen generations, pointing toward the birth of Jesus.

Verses 18-25 – Jesus' birth was supernatural:

a) He was born of a virgin.

b) The birth was foretold.

c) Angelic announcements accompanied His birth.

d) His name spoke of God's redemptive action in Him.

Prayer Focus: Lord, help me to be like Joseph who, even though he couldn't understand exactly what You were doing in his life, was willing to submit to Your will. Amen.

Notes:

Spiritual Journal:

Week: One
Day: Tuesday
Book: Matthew
Chapter: Two
Memory Verse: Six
Principle: God has a way of protecting His own even when everyone else may suffer.
Outline:

> Verses 1-3 – The wise men come to Herod seeking the newborn king of the Jews.
>
> Verses 4-6 – The prophecies of His birthplace are revealed.
>
> Verses 7-11 – The wise men visit the Holy Family in Bethlehem.
>
> Verses 12-15 – The wise men and the Holy Family are supernaturally warned and escape.
>
> Verses 16-18 – Herod slaughters the innocent children.
>
> Verses 19-23 – The Holy Family returns to the Holy Land.

Prayer Focus: Lord, may I always be sensitive to Your directions so that I can remain safe in Your protective arms. Amen.

Notes:

Spiritual Journal:

Week: One
Day: Wednesday
Book: Matthew
Chapter: Three
Memory Verse: Seventeen
Principle: Jesus' person and ministry are supernaturally approved.
Outline:

       Verses 1-12 – John the Baptist's ministry:

             a) His message was repentance.

             b) He proclaimed judgment.

             c) He announced the coming of the Messiah.

             d) He characterized the Messiah's ministry as one of anointing and purging.

       Verses 13-15 – John baptized Jesus.

       Verses 16-17 – God put His stamp of approval upon Jesus.

             a) The Holy Spirit appeared.

             b) The Father proclaimed that Jesus was His beloved Son and that He was well pleased with Him.

Prayer Focus: Lord, help me to be willing to allow the Messiah to baptize me in the Holy Spirit and to be totally purged of all the chaff in my life.   Amen.

Notes:

Spiritual Journal:

Week: One

Day: Thursday

Book: Matthew

Chapter: Four

Memory Verse: Nineteen

Principle: The call of God separated His men from their natural conditions. Jesus was separated into the desert for forty days and nights, the disciples were separated from their natural professions, and the afflicted were separated from their diseases and demonic torments.

Outline:

Verses 1-11 – Jesus was confronted by Satan:

a) Satan challenged Jesus with the question of whether He really was the Son of God.

b) He was tempted in the *physical* realm to make food for Himself after the forty-day fast.

c) He was tempted in the *soulical* realm to throw Himself from the pinnacle of the Temple.

d) He was tempted in the *spiritual* realm to worship Satan.

e) Each time, Jesus confronted the tempter with the Word of God.

Verses 12-17 – Jesus traveled to the Galilee area and began to preach.

Verses 18-22 – Jesus began to select His disciples.

Verses 23-25 – Because His ministry was accompanied with miracle manifestations, great crowds followed Him.

Prayer Focus: Lord, help me to hide Your Word in my heart so that I will not sin against You, and help me to rightly understand Your Word so that I will not be tricked if it is presented to me with a false intent. Amen.

Notes:

Spiritual Journal:

Week: One
Day: Friday
Book: Matthew
Chapter: Five
Memory Verse: Sixteen
Principle: In the Sermon on the Mount, Jesus teaches us true spirituality which comes from the heart rather than superficial religious practices.
Outline:

> Verses 1-2 – Introduction
>
> Verses 3-12 – The Beatitudes
>
> Verses 13-16 – Christians are to have a positive impact on the world around them as salt and light do on their environments.
>
> Verses 17-20 – Jesus came to fulfill the Old Testament Law.
>
> Verses 21-47 – Jesus gave a new interpretation to the Old Testament regulations: the spirit versus the letter:
>
> a) On murder
>
> b) On giving
>
> c) On civil actions
>
> d) On adultery
>
> e) On divorce
>
> f) On vows
>
> g) On retaliation
>
> h) On neighbors and enemies
>
> Verse 48 – We are called to be perfect just as God Himself is perfect.

Prayer Focus: Lord, help me to have the perfect and true love of God inside of me and to let it flow out to all around me. Keep me from falling into religion rather than really manifesting Your love. Amen.

Notes:

Spiritual Journal:

Week: Two

Day: Monday

Book: Matthew

Chapter: Six

Memory Verse: Thirty-three

Principle: This portion of the Sermon on the Mount deals with checking our motives to ensure that we are motivated by a genuine love for God rather than a religious desire to be seen by people.

Outline:

Verses 1-4 – Almsgiving

Verses 5-8 – Prayer

Verses 9-13 – The Lord's Prayer

Verses 14-15 – Forgiveness

Verses 16-18 – Fasting

Verses 19-21 – True treasures

Verses 22-23 – Living in God's light

Verse 24 – Serving one master

Verses 25-33 – Relying upon God rather than natural resources

Verse 34 – Trusting God for the future

Prayer Focus: Lord, help me to understand the value of true spirituality and to treasure it and to disregard the recognition and possessions which the world considers of worth. Amen.

Notes:

Spiritual Journal:

Week: Two
Day: Tuesday
Book: Matthew
Chapter: Seven
Memory Verse: Twelve
Principle: In this chapter, Jesus gives us a teaching on internal attitudes and external actions which will guarantee our entrance into the narrow gate of heaven.
Outline:

Verses 1-2 – Judging others opens the door for our own judgment.

Verses 3-5 – Cautions against hypocrisy

Verse 6 – This unusual verse is usually interpreted as a warning not to talk about spiritual things to unspiritual people. However, it could be a follow-up to the teaching on hypocrisy in that Jesus may be quoting the current philosophy of the religious leaders of the day. If so, Jesus is showing how they are proclaiming themselves holier than others.

Verses 7-11 – God's promise to always answer all sorts of prayers

Verse 12 – The Golden Rule

Verses 13-14 – The carefully defined entrance into heaven versus the careless road to hell

Verses 15-23 – A person's true self is revealed by how he lives, not by what he claims to be.

Verses 24-27 – Our future is determined by the foundation upon which we build our lives.

Verses 28-29 – The authority behind Jesus' teaching set Him apart from other religious leaders of His time.

Prayer Focus: Lord, help me to have a genuineness on the inside which shows clearly on the outside. Amen.

Notes:

Spiritual Journal:

Week: Two
Day: Wednesday
Book: Matthew
Chapter: Eight
Memory Verse: Seventeen
Principle: In this chapter, Jesus demonstrated not only the power of God in that He healed a number of people and set many free from demonic power, but He also demonstrated God's graciousness and love in ministering to the unaccepted elements of society: gentiles, an officer of an occupation military force, women, lepers, demoniacs, and faithless disciples.

Outline:
 Verses 1-4 – The leper
 Verses 5-13 – The officer of the occupation military force
 Verses 14-15 – The women
 Verses 16-17 – The prophetic nature of His ministry
 Verses 18-22 – Jesus laid out extreme requirements of discipleship.
 Verses 23-27 – Calming the storm at sea for the faithless disciples
 Verses 28-34 – Delivering the demoniac of Gergesa

Prayer Focus: Lord, help me to focus on Your love and graciousness as well as Your power. Help me to see the value of everyone around me rather than to try, through my human prejudice, to determine his worth. Amen.

Notes:

Spiritual Journal:

Week: Two
Day: Thursday
Book: Matthew
Chapter: Nine
Memory Verse: Thirty-six

Principle: In this chapter, Jesus was confronted by religious tradition which would have squeezed out the life of God and replaced it with the deadness of human tradition, if possible.

Outline:

Verses 1-8 – Jesus was called a blasphemer because He proclaimed that the man's sins were forgiven.

Verses 9-13 – Jesus was ridiculed because He called a publican as a disciple and ate with his friends.

Verses 14-15 – Jesus was challenged because His disciples were not practicing the religious "duty" of fasting.

Verses 16-17 – Jesus explained that the new life which we have in Him is spoiled, not helped, by trying to patch in the old religious traditions.

Verses 18-26 – Jesus healed the woman with the issue of blood and raised the dead girl. Each of these stories, in addition to demonstrating the love and power of God, symbolically represent the struggle portrayed in the rest of the chapter. In both cases, there was physical contact with persons considered to be unclean. The woman had grown worse by following all the traditional treatments. The followers of the traditional mourning custom laughed at Jesus and had to be put out of the room.

Verses 27-31 – The healing of the two blind men showed that the recovery came by faith, not by any religious practice.

Verses 32-34 – The religious leaders accused Jesus of using demonic power.

Verses 35-38 – Jesus demonstrated that He was motivated by compassion and a desire to draw men into the Kingdom of God.

Prayer Focus: Lord, help me to see people clearly through Your eyes and not through the dirty glasses of religion and tradition. Amen.

Notes:

Spiritual Journal:

Week: Two
Day: Friday
Book: Matthew
Chapter: Ten
Memory Verse: Thirty-eight
Principle: This section focuses on the urgency of the mission for believers to share the gospel with the world.
Outline:

Verse 1 – Jesus empowered the disciples before He commissioned them.

Verses 2-4 – Jesus named His original twelve disciples.

Verses 5-6 – Limited scope of the initial mission

Verses 7-8 – The plan of operation for mission work

Verses 9-10 – The disciples were to learn to live by faith in that they were not permitted to carry any material provision for the mission.

Verses 11-15 – Blessing and cursing upon those who receive or reject

Verses 16-31 – Preparation for opposition and encouragement that they should not fear or be turned away from the mission because of threats or attacks

Verses 32-33 – Promise to the ones who confess the Lord and curse to those who deny Him

Verses 34-37 – The issue of the gospel will override the deepest of loyalties.

Verses 38-39 – Life-and-death nature of accepting the gospel

Verses 40-42 – Rewards for those who receive Christ's messengers

Prayer Focus: Lord, let me realize the true urgency of the mission You have left with Your disciples. Amen.

Notes:

Spiritual Journal:

Week: Three
Day: Monday
Book: Matthew
Chapter: Eleven
Memory Verse: Twenty-eight
Principle: The guiding principle of this chapter is that the ones most likely to understand the truth are often the ones who miss it. Even John the Baptist, who had announced Jesus' coming, questioned his own proclamation.
Outline:
Verse 1 – Narrative concerning Jesus' movements
Verses 2-6 – John the Baptist questioned Jesus' messiahship and was answered by being reminded of the works Jesus was performing.
Verses 7-15 – Jesus commended John's ministry and person.
Verses 16-19 – Jesus addressed the inconsistencies of the people: nothing pleased them, and they found fault with everything.
Verses 20-24 – Jesus addressed the judgment pending on the cities which rejected His ministry.
Verses 25-27 – Knowledge of God is by revelation.
Verses 28-30 – Jesus invites us to come to Him and receive His yoke and burden.
Prayer Focus: Lord, help me to receive your revelation and not to be discouraged from having faith and trust in You. Let me take Your yoke and burden. Amen.
Notes:

Spiritual Journal:

Week: Three
Day: Tuesday
Book: Matthew
Chapter: Twelve
Memory Verse: Thirty-six

Principle: In this chapter, Jesus dealt with people's heart attitudes. Some were religious about Sabbath observance, but their hearts were evil. Some openly blasphemed Jesus because of their evil hearts. Some were "spiritual" (wanting to see signs), but their hearts were wicked. One was even delivered of demonic activity but allowed the possession to return because his heart was empty. Even Jesus' own family was evaluated.

Outline:

Verses 1-8 – The Pharisees questioned Jesus concerning plucking corn on the Sabbath.
   a) Jesus answered that David ate the shewbread.
   b) Jesus answered that the priests work on the Sabbath.
   c) Jesus is greater than the Temple.
   d) Jesus is Lord of the Sabbath.

Verses 9-13 – The healing of the man with the withered hand
   a) The Pharisees questioned Jesus as to whether it was right to heal on the Sabbath.
   b) Jesus tells a parable about the sheep in the well.
   c) The man was healed.

Verses 14-21 – Jesus' reaction to the plot of the Pharisees
   a) The Pharisees devised a plot.
   b) Jesus avoided the public, but they pursued Him.
   c) His compassion on the multitude was prophetic.

Verses 22-30 – The Pharisees claimed that Jesus' ministry was of Beelzebub.
   a) A deaf and dumb boy was healed.
   b) The Pharisees' accusation
   c) The house divided

Verses 31-32 – Blasphemy against the Holy Ghost

Verses 33-37 – The power of good words and of bad ones

Verses 38-40 – Jesus refused to give the Jews a sign.

Verses 41-42 – Condemnation of the generation

Verses 43-44 – Unclean spirits return

Verses 45-50 – Jesus' true family

Prayer Focus: Lord, remake my heart to be a pure source out of which good fruit for You can grow. Amen.

Notes and Spiritual Journal:

Week: Three
Day: Wednesday
Book: Matthew
Chapter: Thirteen
Memory Verse: Forty-six
Principle: The truths of the Kingdom of Heaven are hidden inside the hearts of believers
    and bring forth the manifestation of the Kingdom of God.
Outline:
    Verses 1-23 – The parable of the sower
        a) Parables are given because the heart, ears, and eyes of some people are
            closed to the truth.
        b) The seed is the Word of God.
        c) The types of soil picture the hearts of men.
            1) The soil of the wayside is the heart that doesn't understand.
            2) The stony soil is the heart of the one with no depth of
               comprehension.
            3) The weedy soil is the heart with too many other concerns.
            4) The good soil is the heart which is productive with the Word of
               God.
    Verses 24-30 – The parable of the tares of the field illustrates that the devil will
        infiltrate with evil individuals, but God will sort them out for judgment.
    Verses 31-32 – The parable of the mustard seed illustrates that the Kingdom of
        Heaven is an almost unnoticeable force which produces inestimable
        results.
    Verse 33 – The parable of the leaven reiterates the secret power of the Kingdom,
        which works under cover and unnoticed to bring about its result.
    Verses 34-35 – The power of parables is to reveal the secrets of the Kingdom of
        God.
    Verses 36-43 – Jesus explained the parable of the tares of the field.
    Verse 44 – The parable of the buried treasure
    Verses 45-46 – The parable of the pearl of great price
    Verses 47-50 – The parable of the net and the mixed catch of fish
    Verses 51-52 – The parable of the old and new treasures
    Verses 53-58 – The Jews took offense with Jesus because they could not believe
        that He was more than a normal human being.
Prayer Focus: Lord, help me to receive the powerful secrets of the Word of God as seed
    into my heart so that I may produce abundantly in Your Kingdom.   Amen.
Notes and Spiritual Journal:

Week: Three
Day: Thursday
Book: Matthew
Chapter: Fourteen
Memory Verse: Twenty-seven
Principle: Jesus ministers to all of man's needs: He feeds the physically hungry multitude, and He comforts the emotionally fearful disciples in the tempest.
Outline:
       Verses 1-12 – Herod beheads John the Baptist.
       Verses 13-14 – Jesus' compassion brings Him back into the eye of the public to heal the sick.
       Verses 15-21 – Jesus multiplies five loaves and two fish to feed a multitude.
       Verses 22-33 – Jesus walks on the stormy sea and calms not only the wind and waves but also the hearts of His disciples.
       Verses 34-36 – Jesus heals many in the gentile region.
Prayer Focus: Lord, help me not to be fearful or unbelieving or of little faith but to always realize that You are there in the middle of all my needs.   Amen.
Notes:

Spiritual Journal:

Week: Three
Day: Friday
Book: Matthew
Chapter: Fifteen
Memory Verse: Eleven
Principle: This chapter continues a theme which runs throughout the book: the internal versus the external. He shows that evil in the heart is the corrupting factor and that even those who might not be accepted because of external conditions such as ethnic background are candidates for God's blessings.
Outline:
> Verses 1-9 – Jesus answered the challenges of the Jews by showing them that they are guilty of internal sin.
>
> Verses 10-20 – Jesus explained the corrupting effects of an evil heart.
>
> Verses 21-28 – Jesus delivered the daughter of a gentile woman who would normally be considered as unworthy of a miracle from God.
>
> Verses 29-39 – Jesus miraculously fed the multitude of four thousand. These were gentiles who were traditionally considered defiled, but Jesus blessed them anyway.

Prayer Focus: Lord, help me to have Your wisdom and insight to see the corruption in my own heart and the boldness to allow You to deal with it. Amen.
Notes:

Spiritual Journal:

Week: Four
Day: Monday
Book: Matthew
Chapter: Sixteen
Memory Verse: Twenty-six

Principle: In this section, Jesus draws our attention to the internal revelation of the Kingdom of God. The Jews seek a visible sign, but He offers them a spiritual one. The disciples are concerned about physical bread when Jesus talks to them about spiritual leaven. He is looking for spiritual revelation of His identity while the disciples are offering suggestions based on physical observations. Peter reacts to the physical rather than the spiritual implications of the coming crucifixion. Jesus teaches about the soul versus tangible possessions.

Outline:

 Verses 1-4 – Jesus declared a sign from heaven to confirm His identity.

 Verses 5-12 – Jesus declared the danger of the doctrines and unbelief of the Pharisees.

 Verses 13-18 – Jesus tested the disciples to see if they had a revelation of His identity and showed them that such a revelation is foundational to the church.

 Verses 19-20 – The keys to the Kingdom

 Verses 21-23 – Peter misunderstands the message of the coming crucifixion.

 Verses 24-26 – The way to salvation of the soul is denial of the physical life.

 Verses 27-28 – Prophecy of the physical coming of the spiritual kingdom

Prayer Focus: Lord, help me to be wise enough to recognize the cross so that I can take it up and to be humble enough to lay down my own life so that I can follow after You. Amen.

Notes:

Spiritual Journal:

Week: Four

Day: Tuesday

Book: Matthew

Chapter: Seventeen

Memory Verse: Twenty

Principle: Failing to maintain a faith-filled life is actually rebelliousness; Jesus addressed His disciples as being "perverse" when they were not able to function in the supernatural ability which He had given them in chapter ten.

Outline:

Verses 1-9 – The transfiguration shows the association of Jesus with the Old Testament Law (represented by Moses) and the prophets (represented by Elijah). Peter suggested that three tabernacles be built to honor the three, but God responded by teaching a lesson. By removing the two Old Testament figures and proclaiming Jesus to be His son and by commanding that the disciples hear Him, God proved Christ's superiority to the Old Testament.

Verses 10-13 – John the Baptist as Elijah

Verses 14-18 – The lunatic boy delivered and the disciples scolded for their lack of faith

Verses 19-21 – Admonition on having and exercising true faith

Verses 22-23 – Prophecy of the crucifixion

Verses 24-27 – The miracle of the coin in the fish's mouth

Prayer Focus: Lord, help me never to lose the faith that You have given me but to exercise it so that it ever increases. Amen.

Notes:

Spiritual Journal:

Week: Four
Day: Wednesday
Book: Matthew
Chapter: Eighteen
Memory Verse: Three
Principle: This section of scripture deals with offenses: first, Jesus shows the disciples the offensiveness of pride; then, He teaches on offenses against the little ones in the Kingdom of God; next, He addresses the issues of holding or loosing offenses and explains the extent to which we must loose others from offenses; finally, He compares our level of forgiveness with the magnanimous forgiveness of God toward us.

Outline:

Verses 1-4 – Those who have faith as a little child are the greatest in the Kingdom of God.

Verses 5-10 – Judgment against those who offend the little ones in God's Kingdom

a) Offenses in general, but especially those against the little ones in the Kingdom, are under God's judgment.

b) The issue of cutting off the offending hand and gouging out the offending eye must be seen in light of what Jesus had already taught concerning the source of evil being in the heart of man, not in his physical members.

Verses 11-14 – Seeking the one lost sheep

Verses 15-17 – Confronting the trespasser

Verses 18-22 – The believer's responsibility to forgive multiple times rather than to hold others bound by their offenses

Verses 23-35 – Judgment upon those who are unforgiving in light of the forgiveness they have received

Prayer Focus: Lord, help me to live free from holding on to and from giving offense. Amen.

Notes:

Spiritual Journal:

Week: Four

Day: Thursday

Book: Matthew

Chapter: Nineteen

Memory Verse: Fourteen

Principle: This chapter is actually two different sections with separate themes: the covenant relationship of marriage, which God expects His people to uphold, and the attitudes and actions necessary to enter the Kingdom.

Outline:

        Verses 1-2 – Jesus healed the multitudes.

        Verses 3-9 – When the Jews tempted Jesus concerning Moses' teachings on divorce, He responded with an explanation from the order of creation: that man is responsible to uphold his marriage covenant and that breaking it was a punishable offense against the Kingdom.

        Verses 10-12 – Not everyone is able to remain celibate.

        Verses 13-15 – The Kingdom of Heaven is made up of those with hearts like little children.

        Verses 16-22 – The rich man was challenged to receive the treasures of heaven by giving up the treasures of earth.

        Verses 23-26 – Entering the Kingdom of Heaven by one's own worth is impossible for even the rich; entrance into heaven is possible only through God.

        Verses 27-30 – He extended a promise of reward for all who sacrifice the physical to gain the spiritual.

Prayer Focus: Lord, help me to always see beyond the immediate and to be able to bring the eternal into focus. Amen.

Notes:

Spiritual Journal:

Week: Four
Day: Friday
Book: Matthew
Chapter: Twenty
Memory Verse: Twenty-seven
Principle: Entrance into a position in the Kingdom of God is not based on works but upon
      God's grace alone.
Outline:
> Verses 1-16 – The parable of the vineyard workers proves that merit in the Kingdom of Heaven is not earned but is a free gift based on God's graciousness.
>
> Verses 17-19 – Another prophecy of the coming crucifixion
>
> Verses 20-23 – Jesus' answer to the request by John and James' mother that they be recognized in the Kingdom accentuated the fact that position is not a reward.
>
> Verses 24-28 – Jesus taught the disciples that position in the Kingdom was gained by service, not dominion.
>
> Verses 29-34 – The healing of two blind men demonstrates that those whom natural men would not recognize are the ones in line for God's blessings.

Prayer Focus: Lord, help me to be willing to be the last and help me to be willing to serve – not so that I can advance in Your Kingdom, but so that I can truly be like You. Amen.

Notes:

Spiritual Journal:

Week: Five
Day: Monday
Book: Matthew
Chapter: Twenty-one
Memory Verse: Twenty-two
Principle: This passage demonstrates the fruitlessness of the religious system of the time: even though people proclaimed Jesus as the Messiah at the Triumphal Entry, the same people will call for His crucifixion within the week; they had turned the Temple into a house of commerce rather than a place of true worship; just like the fig tree, they had pretentious leaves but no real fruit; the questions which the religious leaders asked Jesus were not for information but to try to entrap Him; Jesus' parables showed that those who were placed in position were self-seeking rather than taking responsible care of their duties.

Outline:
    Verses 1-11 – The Triumphal Entry
        a) Supernatural revelation of how to find a donkey
        b) Rejoicing of the people at Jesus' coming
        c) Singing of messianic psalms
    Verses 12-16 – Cleansing of the Temple
    Verses 17-20 – The cursing of the fig tree was not an act of anger on Jesus' part but a prophetic act using the Old Testament symbol of the fig tree (representing Israel) to show the judgment awaiting them because of their spiritual barrenness.
    Verses 21-22 – Jesus demonstrated two truths in His answer to the disciples concerning the fig tree:
        a) He used the symbolism of the mountain as the nation of Israel and the sea as the peoples of the earth to prophesy about the coming expulsion of the people of Israel out of the Holy Land.
        b) He taught them about the power of their faith.
    Verses 23-27 – Jesus outwitted His tempters.
    Verses 28-41 – Two parables unveil the evil of the religious leaders.
        a) The story of the two sons shows that they claimed to be doing the Father's will but were actually rebelling against it.
        b) The parable of the vineyard keepers revealed their self-seeking motivations.
    Verses 42-46 – Hypocrisy will not go without being judged.
Prayer Focus: Lord, purge me of hypocrisy – intentional and unintentional: that of which I am aware and that which is secret even to me. Amen.
Notes and Spiritual Journal:

Week: Five
Day: Tuesday
Book: Matthew
Chapter: Twenty-two
Memory Verse: Twenty-one
Principle: This chapter follows the previous one in dealing with the deceitfulness and deadliness of hypocrisy.

Outline:

Verses 1-14 – The parable of the wedding feast illustrates the religious leaders' resistance to God's call and His openness to the irreligious who will accept His call. It also illustrates His rejection of the hypocrite who tries to get into the Kingdom without being changed.

Verses 15-22 – The question of the tribute money illustrates the hypocrisy of the Pharisees and the Herodians, who were arch-enemies with different opinions concerning paying tribute to Rome; they united in an attempt to trap Jesus.

Verses 23-33 – The question about the resurrection was another hypocritical challenge raised by the Sadducees, who did not believe in the resurrection.

Verses 34-40 – The lawyer's question about the greatest commandment was his attempt to trap Jesus into placing one of the Ten Commandments above the others, but Jesus proved that the principles of God are greater than the laws of God.

Verses 41-46 – Jesus turned the tables on the religious leaders by asking them a question which would have entrapped them if they dared to answer.

Prayer Focus: Lord, I need to have my heart and mind searched to see if there is any evil thought or intent; purify me of anything that is not acceptable in Your sight. Amen.

Notes:

Spiritual Journal:

Week: Five
Day: Wednesday
Book: Matthew
Chapter: Twenty-three
Memory Verse: Eleven
Principle: Having determined the errors of hypocrisy, Jesus now turns to the judgments pending on those who practice it.
Outline:
        Verses 1-7 – He warned against following the practices of the corrupt religious leaders.
        Verses 8-12 – The path to exaltation is the way of humility.
        Verses 13-33 – The characteristics of the hypocrites and the woes awaiting them
        Verses 34-39 – Jesus reminds those deserving of judgment that He has given them opportunities to repent and be restored, but they refused.
Prayer Focus: Lord, don't let me fail to take advantage of the opportunities You give me to receive Your restoration.   Amen.
Notes:

Spiritual Journal:

Week: Five
Day: Thursday
Book: Matthew
Chapter: Twenty-four
Memory Verse: Forty-four
Principle: Since no one knows the day of the Lord's return, we must live each day in a state of readiness.
Outline:

Verses 1-3 – Jesus initiates a prophetic discourse, and the disciples ask Him to give them some clues as to the timing of future events.

Verses 4-8 – Jesus gives some signs which will happen but will not necessarily indicate the end of the age.
a) Deceivers
b) Wars
c) Pestilence
d) Earthquakes

Verses 9-14 – Signs which do indicate the end
a) Persecution and betrayal of believers
b) False prophets
c) Iniquity
d) World-wide evangelism

Verses 15-22 – The sign that it is too late
a) The abomination of desolation
b) The urgency of the situation
c) God's promise to shorten the days

Verses 23-27 – Warning not to be deceived by claims of the false messiah

Verses 28-31 – Results of the prophetic events
a) Gathering of the saints
b) Universal upheaval
c) The appearing of the Lord

Verses 32-33 – The fig tree parable represents a rebirth of the nation of Israel.

Verse 34 – The generation which witnesses the signs will also witness the event.

Verse 35 – Assurance that the promise will be fulfilled

Verses 36-51 – Admonition to be vigilant
a) No one knows the exact time.
b) Life will go on until the unexpected events overtake.
c) Some will be ready; some will not.
d) Be watchful to prevent being caught defenseless.
e) The faithful will be rewarded, but the slothful will be judged.

Prayer Focus: Lord, help me to be focused on You and Your work of seeing that the gospel of the Kingdom is preached worldwide; don't let me become fearful, unbelieving, or slothful in the last days.   Amen.

Notes and Spiritual Journal:

Week: Five
Day: Friday
Book: Matthew
Chapter: Twenty-five
Memory Verse: Forty
Principle: At the final judgment, the hidden differences between the faithful and the unfaithful (virgins with oil and those without, stewards who have done the master's will and those who have failed, sheep and goats) will be manifested.
Outline:
>Verses 1-13 – The parable of the ten virgins illustrates that there is a need for foresightedness and readiness which goes beyond purity in order to be acceptable to the Bridegroom.
>Verses 14-30 – The parable of the talents teaches us that the Lord expects His disciples to occupy the earth and take active dominion while waiting for His return.
>Verses 31-46 – The parable of the sheep and goats shows us that our actions toward other humans reveal the true nature of our hearts.
Prayer Focus: Lord, I ask that You reveal the secrets of my heart now while I still have opportunity to deal with them rather than having them exposed at the final judgment when it will be too late. Amen.
Notes:

Spiritual Journal:

Week: Six
Day: Monday
Book: Matthew
Chapter: Twenty-six
Memory Verse: Forty-one
Principle: Jesus willingly presents Himself as mankind's atoning sacrifice, even when He is betrayed and denied by His close friends.
Outline:
        Verses 1-2 – Jesus prophesies His imminent crucifixion.
        Verses 3-5 – The Jews plot Jesus' destruction.
        Verses 6-13 – Jesus is anointed for His impending burial.
        Verses 14-16 – Judas receives a bribe to betray Jesus.
        Verses 17-19 – Miraculous direction is given for preparation of the Last Supper.
        Verses 20-25 – Jesus prophesies His betrayal.
        Verses 26-30 – The communion is instituted.
        Verses 31-35 – The prophecy of Peter's denial and his refusal to believe
        Verses 36-46 – The agony of Jesus in Gethsemane and the disciples' inability to watch with the Lord
        Verses 47-56 – The betrayal by Judas and Jesus' arrest
        Verses 57-68 – Jesus' trial and mocking before the high priest
        Verses 69-75 – Peter's denial and repentance
Prayer Focus: Lord, protect me from denying or betraying You, help me to be willing to receive Your warning when I am in danger of dishonoring You, and help me to be quick to repent when I am wrong.   Amen.
Notes:

Spiritual Journal:

Week: Six

Day: Tuesday

Book: Matthew

Chapter: Twenty-seven

Memory Verse: Thirty-seven

Principle: In this account of the crucifixion, we see the sinlessness of Jesus contrasted with the sinfulness of men, signifying the fulfillment of the Old Testament symbolism of the innocent lamb substituting for guilty humanity.

Outline:

Verses 1-2 – Jesus is taken to the Roman court.

Verses 3-10 – Judas shows remorse over having betrayed the Master but finds no consolation.

Verses 11-26 – Jesus before Pilate

a) Pilate realizes that Jesus is innocent.

b) Pilate tries to get Jesus released by offering Barabbas.

c) The Jews call for the blood guilt of Jesus to be upon themselves and their children.

Verses 27-32 – Jesus is mocked by the Roman soldiers.

a) He is dressed as a king and ridiculed.

b) Simon the Cyrene is compelled to assist Him with the cross.

Verses 33-56 – The crucifixion

a) The mocking name plate is raised above the cross.

b) The observers ridicule Him.

c) Even the others being executed with Him ridicule Him.

d) He cries out, "My God, My God, why have You forsaken Me?"

e) He gives up the spirit.

f) The Temple curtain is ripped, and Old Testament saints are seen in the city of Jerusalem.

g) The centurion recognizes that Jesus was the son of God.

Verses 57-66 – The burial

a) Joseph gives his own tomb to Jesus.

b) The Jews have a watch set to guard the tomb.

Prayer Focus: Lord, help me to always keep the crucifixion as the central focus of my thinking and living.   Amen.

Notes and Spiritual Journal:

Week: Six

Day: Wednesday

Book: Matthew

Chapter: Twenty-eight

Memory Verse: Six

Principle: The meaning of the present chapter may best be summed up in the words of the Apostle Paul, "Death is swallowed up in victory!"

Outline:

> Verses 1-7 – The angel of the Lord appeared to the women at the tomb early on Easter morning to announce the resurrection.
>
> Verses 8-10 – Jesus appeared to the women and commissioned them to tell the disciples about the resurrection.
>
> Verses 11-15 – The guards and the Jewish council devised a plot to cover up the evidence of the resurrection.
>
> Verses 16-20 – The Great Commission

Prayer Focus: Lord, help me to constantly realize and manifest the victory You won when You rose from the dead. Amen.

Notes:

Spiritual Journal:

Week: Six

Day: Thursday

Book: Mark

Chapter: One

Memory Verse: Forty-one

Principle: I John says that the Son of God was manifested that He might destroy the works of the devil; this chapter proves the point.

Outline:

       Verses 1-8 – John the Baptist is a forerunner announcing the coming of Jesus.

       Verses 9-11 – The Father affirms the Son at the baptism by John.

       Verses 12-13 – The temptation

       Verses 14-20 – Jesus begins to collect His disciples.

       Verses 21-37 – Jesus ministers in Capernaum.

           a) His doctrine is astonishing to the people.

           b) The deliverance of the demoniac in the synagogue

           c) Peter's mother-in-law is healed.

           d) Many are healed and delivered.

           e) Jesus' personal prayer time with the Father

       Verses 38-45 – The ministry expands to other towns and cities.

           a) Demons are cast out.

           b) The leper is healed.

           c) His fame is published abroad.

           d) Jesus retreats to a private place, but is followed by the multitude.

Prayer Focus: Lord, help me to constantly be aware of and dependent upon Your presence to destroy the works of the devil in my life and the lives of those around me. Amen.

Notes:

Spiritual Journal:

Week: Six
Day: Friday
Book: Mark
Chapter: Two
Memory Verse: Twenty-two

Principle: This chapter encourages us to look beyond the physical and to see the spiritual aspects of life: beyond physical sickness, we see spiritual sinfulness; beyond men's occupations or religious affiliations, we see their heart conditions; beyond religious practices, we see the internal motivations and relationships.

Outline:

Verses 1-12 – The healing of the man with the palsy proves that Jesus was just as much the forgiver of sins as He was the healer of bodies.

Verses 13-17 – Jesus accepts the publicans and sinners.

a) Levi, the tax collector, was called as a disciple.

b) Jesus eats with publicans and sinners.

c) Jesus defended His association with them.

Verses 18-20 – When the Pharisees question the disciples about fasting, Jesus explains the true meaning of fasting and its spiritual relationship.

Verses 21-22 – The parables of the new wine and the torn garment prove that the Kingdom of God is a totally new relationship with God, not a patched-up version of the old legalism.

Verses 23-28 – When the disciples ate corn that they plucked on the Sabbath, Jesus explained that the Sabbath was made for man, not vice versa.

Prayer Focus: Lord, help me to never try to contain Your new life in my old vessel of natural religion.   Amen.

Notes:

Spiritual Journal:

Week: Seven
Day: Monday
Book: Mark
Chapter: Three
Memory Verse: Fifteen
Principle: After the miracle-working power of Jesus is re-emphasized, Jesus passes it on to His disciples and then declares that those who obey His will are His true family.
Outline:
Verses 1-6 – The healing of the man's withered hand demonstrated that it was lawful to do good works on the Sabbath day.
Verses 7-12 – Jesus healed and delivered the multitudes.
Verses 13-19 – The disciples were appointed and anointed.
Verses 20-27 – Two reactions to His ministry
a) The multitudes loved Him and sought after Him.
b) The Jews hated Him and accused Him.
Verses 28-30 – Jesus explained the unforgivable sin.
Verses 31-35 – Jesus defined the ones who do His will as His true family.
Prayer Focus: Lord, I want to be part of Your true family; help me to receive Your power and fulfill Your will.   Amen.
Notes:

Spiritual Journal:

Week: Seven
Day: Tuesday
Book: Mark
Chapter: Four
Memory Verse: Forty
Principle: The Kingdom of Heaven is easily revealed in the acts of God in the natural order around us; with proper faith and insight, we can see God's hand at work in every aspect of creation.
Outline:
Verses 1-20 – The parable of the sower explains how our hearts determine how much fruit the Word of God will produce in our lives.
Verses 21-34 – Other parables reveal the nature of the Kingdom of Heaven.
a) The candle parable tells us that the nature of the Kingdom is to share God's light with the dark world.
b) The parable of the wheat shows us that God is at work secretly even when we can't see that He is doing anything.
c) The parable of the mustard seed shows the inestimable power of the Kingdom.
Verses 35-41 – The story of the calming of the storm at sea shows us that with fearless faith, we can see God's miracle provision in even the worst of conditions.
Prayer Focus: Lord, help me to always realize the inestimable power of the Kingdom which is working on my behalf even when I don't see it; help me to remember that You are always in the boat with me, even when the storms are raging.   Amen.
Notes:

Spiritual Journal:

Week: Seven
Day: Wednesday
Book: Mark
Chapter: Five
Memory Verse: Thirty-six
Principle: Jesus has the solution to every problem of every area of our lives: He set the demoniac free from possession in his spirit-man, He brought physical healing to the woman with the issue of blood and to Jairus' daughter, and He calmed the emotional fears and worry of Jairus and his wife.
Outline:

Verses 1-20 – The deliverance of the demoniac

a) The wild man fell down before Jesus.

1) The spirits in him recognized who Jesus was.

2) The spirits in him begged that Jesus not torment them.

b) Jesus delivered the man and sent the spirits into the pigs.

c) The local community marveled at the event and expelled Jesus from their region.

d) The man wanted to join Jesus, but the Master commanded him to remain in the area and tell the story of his deliverance.

Verses 21-43 – Two miraculous blessings

a) As Jesus was on His way to heal Jairus' daughter, a woman with an issue of blood exercised her faith for healing.

1) She received a healing from Jesus even without a conscious effort on Jesus' part.

2) The disciples contested with Jesus because of the multitude of people around Him; this confrontation tells us that many people were touching Jesus, but only one touched Him with faith.

b) Jairus' daughter was raised from the dead.

1) During the delay caused by the healing of the woman, news came that the girl had died.

2) Jesus confronted the emotional reactions of the parents.

3) He got rid of all except those individuals with true faith – including some of His own disciples as well as the mourners at the funeral.

4) The girl was raised with a word from the Master.

Prayer Focus: Lord, help me to know how to trust You with every area of my being. Amen.
Notes and Spiritual Journal:

Week: Seven
Day: Thursday
Book: Mark
Chapter: Six
Memory Verse: Six
Principle: The focus of this chapter is on the unbelief of men: the people from Jesus' hometown did not believe that Jesus was anything more than an ordinary human being; Herod couldn't believe his own heart concerning John the Baptist; some of the cities of the region rejected the witness of the disciples because of their inability to believe; and even the disciples lacked the faith to believe when they were confronted with the need to feed the multitude and to endure or to subdue the storm.

Outline:

        Verses 1-6 – Jesus is rejected by the citizens of His own hometown.

        Verses 7-13 – The disciples are sent out to evangelize the towns and villages of Israel.

        Verses 14-29 – Herod beheads John the Baptist.

        Verses 30-44 – Jesus feeds the multitude.

        Verses 45-52 – Jesus walks on water and calms the storm.

        Verses 53-56 – Jesus does many miracles in the gentile region of Gennesaret.

Prayer Focus: Lord, my prayer is the same as that of the demon-possessed boy's father: "Lord, I believe; help my unbelief"!   Amen.

Notes:

Spiritual Journal:

Week: Seven
Day: Friday
Book: Mark
Chapter: Seven
Memory Verse: Fifteen
Principle: Things are not always as they seem; when God looks on the heart rather than on the outside, as men do, the real nature of things is revealed.
Outline:
> Verses 1-13 – When the religious Jews challenge Jesus' disciples concerning not keeping the traditional customs, Jesus answers them with a condemnation of their hypocrisy.
>
> Verses 14-23 – Jesus explains that the evil in men's lives is what is in their heart, not what shows externally.
>
> Verses 24-30 – Jesus delivers the daughter of a gentile woman – an individual who, if judged by external standards, would have been rejected rather than helped.
>
> Verses 31-37 – Jesus performed many miracles among the gentiles. These gentiles would have suffered had they been left to be judged by Jewish religious standards.

Prayer Focus: Lord, help me to see with your x-ray vision what is in my own heart and to look through Your eyes when I would want to judge others. Amen.
Notes:

Spiritual Journal:

Week: Eight
Day: Monday
Book: Mark
Chapter: Eight
Memory Verse: Thirty-four
Principle: A good portion of this chapter deals with the issue of sign-dependent faith: the people who were not looking for a sign were given one when the four thousand were miraculously fed; the ones who wanted a sign were denied; the ones who did have a sign couldn't recognize it because they still didn't recognize Jesus' authority even after having seen Him multiply bread on two occasions; Jesus forbade the ones upon whom He did perform signs to show them off; and when Jesus tried to give His disciples a sign of His coming death, they blatantly refused it.
Outline:
        Verses 1-9 – The feeding of the four thousand
        Verses 10-13 – Jesus refuses to give the Pharisees a sign.
        Verses 14-21 – The disciples still are not able to understand the authority of Christ even after having seen His sign ministry.
        Verses 22-26 – Jesus touches a blind man the second time to give him a total healing.
        Verses 27-33 – Peter has a revelation of Jesus' identity, but still falls into deception concerning His mission.
        Verses 34-38 – The cost of discipleship is explained.
Prayer Focus: Lord, help me to be enough like Peter to realize who You are. Help me to not fall short of recognizing and of embracing Your mission as well.   Amen.
Notes:

Spiritual Journal:

Week: Eight
Day: Tuesday
Book: Mark
Chapter: Nine
Memory Verse: Twenty-three
Principle: This chapter covers a series of minor topics from the transfiguration to eternal judgment, but the overriding theme seems to be the breaking in of the supernatural order upon the natural – "believe in it and receive it."
Outline:
> Verses 1-10 – The transfiguration proves Jesus' supernatural nature.
>
> Verses 11-13 – The supernatural element of John the Baptist's ministry is revealed.
>
> Verses 14-27 – Conflict in the supernatural realm is demonstrated in the healing of the epileptic boy.
>
> Verses 28-29 – Prayer is the key to entering into the supernatural realm.
>
> Verses 30-31 – Jesus foretells the crucifixion – the event which will establish His supernatural rule on earth.
>
> Verses 32-37 – The law of humility is portrayed as being the authority of the supernatural kingdom.
>
> Verses 38-50 – Jesus expounds on the judgments to be imposed in the supernatural kingdom.

Prayer Focus: Lord, help me to be able to enter into the supernatural kingdom and to live by its rules so as to manifest the Kingdom fully in my life.   Amen.

Notes:

Spiritual Journal:

Week: Eight
Day: Wednesday
Book: Mark
Chapter: Ten
Memory Verse: Forty-five
Principle: This chapter basically focuses on the conflict between the mindset of the natural versus the mentality of the supernatural kingdom.
Outline:
       Verses 1-12 – Conflict over the perception of the marriage covenant
       Verses 13-30 – Conflict over the perception of the importance of money
       Verses 31-45 – Conflict over the perception of position
       Verses 46-52 – Conflict over the perception of priorities
Prayer Focus: Lord, help me to adopt the worldview of the heavenly kingdom and the core belief system of faith.   Amen.
Notes:

Spiritual Journal:

Week: Eight
Day: Thursday
Book: Mark
Chapter: Eleven
Memory Verse: Twenty-three
Principle: The Triumphal Entry, along with the cleansing of the Temple, the cursing of the fig tree, and the confrontation with the religious leaders build a backdrop against which Jesus can teach the disciples about faith and prayer. Certainly, the multitude gave Jesus a glorious welcome, but the rest of the chapter paints a clear picture of the hypocrisy of the people and their leaders. Those who are to get answers to their prayers must really believe – their hearts must agree with their mouths.

Outline:

Verses 1-11 – The Triumphal Entry

Verses 12-14 – The hypocritical fig tree is cursed.

Verses 15-19 – The hypocritical Temple is cleansed.

Verses 20-21 – The fate of the fig tree (and all hypocrites) is revealed.

Verses 22-26 – The reward for prayer prayed with no hypocrisy in the heart of the believer

Verses 27-33 – Jesus enters into conflict with the hypocrisy of the religious leaders.

Prayer Focus: Lord, free me from hypocrisy and double-mindedness. Amen.

Notes:

Spiritual Journal:

Week: Eight
Day: Friday
Book: Mark
Chapter: Twelve
Memory Verse: Thirty-three
Principle: This chapter seems to accentuate teachings revealed in the previous chapter by showing how each segment of the Jewish religious community acted in hypocrisy as they challenged Jesus.
Outline:
Verses 1-12 – Jesus tells a parable which reveals the hearts of the religious leaders; when they recognize that He is speaking about them, they initiate a plan to eliminate Jesus.

Verses 13-17 – The Pharisees and Herodians – natural enemies with diametrically opposing ideas concerning Roman taxation – challenge Jesus with the anticipation that He would play into the hands of one side or the other.

Verses 18-27 – The Sadducees – who did not believe in the resurrection – try to trick Jesus with a question on just this matter.

Verses 28-34 – A scribe tries to get Jesus into a corner by asking which one of the Ten Commandments is more important than the other nine.

Verses 35-44 – Jesus comments on the wickedness of the hearts of the religious community and contrasts the wickedness of their hearts with the sincerity of the heart of the widow.

Prayer Focus: Lord, search my heart and help me know my ways so that I may discern if there is any evil thing in me. Amen.
Notes:

Spiritual Journal:

Week: Nine
Day: Monday
Book: Mark
Chapter: Thirteen
Memory Verse: Thirty-three
Principle: The meaning of this chapter, which deals with the Second Coming of Christ, is summed up in today's memory verse.
Outline:

       Verses 1-4 – The question of prophetic events arises.

       Verses 5-27 – Jesus presents a series of events which would indicate the nearness of His return. These events would also announce the very event of the end of the world as we know it. He cautioned His hearers to take heed to these signs so as to not be misled.

       Verses 28-37 – Jesus commands His followers to watch carefully as they see the time approaching.

Prayer Focus: Lord, help me to live each day as if it were my last one. Amen.
Notes:

Spiritual Journal:

Week: Nine
Day: Tuesday
Book: Mark
Chapter: Fourteen
Memory Verse: Twenty-one
Principle: This chapter contains a little story about a young man who was grabbed on the night of Jesus' arrest; because he was wearing only a cloth loosely tied about him, he wound up running away naked. This story seems to epitomize the message of the chapter: the revealing of the inner selves of the disciples – the revelation of the devotion of the woman in Simon's house and the exposing of traitors in the midst of Jesus' inner circle.

Outline:

Verses 1-9 – An adoring follower anoints Jesus' feet with costly ointment.

Verses 10-21 – Judas' intention to betray Jesus is revealed.

Verses 22-31 – Jesus prophesies the denial by Peter.

Verses 32-42 – The disciples sleep as Jesus agonizes in prayer over the coming crucifixion.

Verses 43-52 – Betrayed by Judas, Jesus is arrested.

Verses 53-65 – Jesus is tried before the chief priest.

Verses 66-72 – Peter denies the Lord three times.

Prayer Focus: Lord, as the coverings are pulled away from my inner self and I wind up as the book of Hebrews proclaims "naked before Him with whom we have to deal," may denial and betrayal not be found in me. Amen.

Notes:

Spiritual Journal:

Week: Nine
Day: Wednesday
Book: Mark
Chapter: Fifteen
Memory Verse: Thirty-seven
Principle: The crucifixion must not be seen as something imposed upon Jesus; He was in spiritual control even as He stood trial (choosing to refuse to answer) and in His death (giving the spirit, not having His life taken from Him).
Outline:

      Verses 1-15 – The trial before Pilate

      Verses 16-21 – The mocking by the soldiers

      Verses 22-41 – The crucifixion

      Verses 42-47 – The burial

Prayer Focus: Lord, help me to have a vision of the love that held You to the cross on my behalf. Amen.
Notes:

Spiritual Journal:

Week: Nine
Day: Thursday
Book: Mark
Chapter: Sixteen
Memory Verse: Seventeen

Principle: Even though it is likely that verses nine through twenty were not in the original text of Mark, there is no reason to doubt the message these verses teach of the transfer of resurrection power to believers.

Outline:

Verses 1-7 – The women are greeted by an empty tomb and an angelic proclamation of the resurrection on the first Easter morning.

Verses 8-14 – Reactions of unbelief and hardness of heart draw a rebuke from the risen Lord.

Verses 15-20 – Jesus not only commissions but also empowers the disciples to go into all the world and preach His gospel.

Prayer Focus: Lord, I want to receive the power to be Your witness. Amen.

Notes:

Spiritual Journal:

Week: Nine
Day: Friday
Book: Luke
Chapter: One
Memory Verse: Sixty-eight
Principle: Luke begins his gospel by demonstrating that the God of impossibilities is at work in the coming of Jesus: barren Elizabeth, well beyond the age of childbearing, gives birth to John the Baptist, and Mary, a virgin, becomes pregnant with Jesus.
Outline:
> Verses 1-4 – Luke's introduction tells why he is writing this gospel.
>
> Verses 5-25 – The unusual circumstances concerning John's conception, including the angelic visitation to Zacharias and his being struck speechless, confirm that John's ministry is to be supernatural.
>
> Verses 26-38 – Gabriel visits Mary to announce that she is to give birth to the Son of God.
>
> Verses 39-56 – Mary visits Elizabeth, and supernatural confirmations attest to the miracles in each of their wombs.
>
> Verses 57-79 – John's birth is accompanied with supernatural confirmations, such as the father's loss of the ability to speak, followed by the giving of a lengthy prophecy concerning both John and Jesus when his speech was restored.
>
> Verse 80 – John's childhood is a time of preparation for his public ministry.

Prayer Focus: Lord, help me to always see Your hand at work in the impossibilities of life. Amen.
Notes:

Spiritual Journal:

Week: Ten
Day: Monday
Book: Luke
Chapter: Two
Memory Verse: Fifty-two
Principle: The theme of this chapter is that Jesus' childhood was a confirmation of and a preparation for His special mission to the human race.
Outline:
Verses 1-20 – Jesus' birth is heralded by angelic messengers, a celestial choir, and the zealous testimonies of the lowly shepherds.

Verses 21-39 – Jesus' dedication is miraculously attested to by Simeon and Anna.

Verses 40-52 – Jesus' childhood years are characterized by consistent physical and spiritual maturing. The story of His out-of-the-normal attachment to the Temple and His activity there at age twelve epitomizes the nature of the boy: He was not so supernatural that the parents would automatically look for Him in the Temple, but He was spiritually inclined to the point that He wondered why they didn't look there sooner.

Prayer Focus: Lord, help me to also grow in wisdom and in favor with God as I grow in stature and in favor with men.   Amen.
Notes:

Spiritual Journal:

Week: Ten
Day: Tuesday
Book: Luke
Chapter: Three
Memory Verse: Twenty-two

Principle: The announcement and baptism by John, accompanied by the heavenly endorsement, set the stage for Jesus' public ministry. The genealogy attests to the human lineage of Jesus; yet it affirms the divine overriding of the natural order by saying that it was *supposed* that Jesus was the son of Joseph.

Outline:

   Verses 1-20 – John the Baptist's ministry is capsulated with the emphasis placed on his message, his foretelling of Jesus, and his imprisonment.

   Verses 21-22 – A cameo in the life of John the Baptist (the baptism of Jesus) is focused on in order to draw it apart from all the rest of his activities, signifying that this is the most important event in his ministry.

   Verses 23-38 – The genealogy portrays both the humanity and the divinity of Jesus.

Prayer Focus: Lord, I know that Jesus is Your Son in whom You are well pleased, but I desire to hear that same affirmation over my own life as well. Amen.

Notes:

Spiritual Journal:

Week: Ten
Day: Wednesday
Book: Luke
Chapter: Four
Memory Verses: Eighteen and nineteen
Principle: Jesus was filled with the Spirit before He entered the desert for the forty days of fasting; but, after those days of temptation, He was empowered by the Spirit. At that point, He could say that the Spirit was upon Him to bring about the needed deliverance.
Outline:

Verses 1-13 – In the temptation of His body, soul, and spirit – Jesus is consistently able to overcome the tempter with the power of the Word of God.

Verses 14-30 – His teaching in the synagogue of Nazareth upsets the townsfolk because they realize that He was accepting the prophet's promises as being related to Himself. He further upsets them by showing them examples of people who missed out on the blessings of God that go to unexpected recipients. They became so angry that they tried to destroy Him, but His life was preserved.

Verses 31-44 – Jesus' words and actions demonstrate the authority and power which are now resident in Him.

Prayer Focus: Lord, may Your Spirit rest upon me as well. Amen.
Notes:

Spiritual Journal:

Week: Ten
Day: Thursday
Book: Luke
Chapter: Five
Memory Verse: Thirty-two
Principle: This section of scripture illustrates the dramatic differences in how people respond to the Lord: we can be so determined to reach Him that we would tear the roof off a building; we can immediately leave everything to follow Him; or we can resist Him, argue with His teachings, and plot ways to get Him out of our lives.
Outline:
    Verses 1-11 – Jesus' use of Peter's boat and the subsequent miraculous catch of fish set the stage for Peter's call and his immediate response to the call.
    Verses 12-16 – Jesus' miracles drew a multitude of followers to Him.
    Verses 17-26 – The healing of the paralytic draws the antagonism of the religious leaders. They consider it blasphemous that Jesus dares to speak to the man's spiritual condition as well as to his physical need.
    Verses 27-32 – Jesus' calling of Levi prompts criticism from the religious community because of the tax collector's questionable background.
    Verses 33-39 – Jesus teaches parables which illustrate that His Kingdom is to consist of totally new creatures in Christ – not just patched-up versions of their old lives.
Prayer Focus: Lord, let me be totally remade in You. Amen.
Notes:

Spiritual Journal:

Week: Ten
Day: Friday
Book: Luke
Chapter: Six
Memory Verse: Thirty-one
Principle: The Sermon on the Plain, along with the other teachings in this chapter, proclaims that the Kingdom of God is manifest in simplicity and humility with genuine obedience to the heart of God.
Outline:
  Verses 1-11 – The religious community misses the simplicity of the truth because they are focusing on the ritual and regulations of the Sabbath.
  Verses 12-16 – Jesus calls His disciples after a night in prayer, not after testing them with religious obligations.
  Verses 17-49 – The Sermon on the Plain includes blessings, woes, and parables which illustrate the contrast between simple truth and religious pretense.
Prayer Focus: Lord, free me from pretense and release me into truth. Amen.
Notes:

Spiritual Journal:

Week: Eleven
Day: Monday
Book: Luke
Chapter: Seven
Memory Verse: Twenty-three

Principle: The theme or principle which Luke addresses in this chapter deals with human reaction to the presence of God in the person of Jesus. As you read the chapter, note the different responses to the ministry of Jesus; there is even a question raised by John the Baptist.

Outline:

Verses 1-10 – The healing of the centurion's servant illustrates great faith in the ministry of Jesus.

Verses 11-18 – The raising from the dead of the widow's son illustrates how some respond to Jesus' ministry with the awe of curious amazement.

Verses 19-23 – John's question illustrates puzzlement or questioning in response to the ministry of Christ.

Verses 24-35 – Jesus confronts the people over their disbelief and hypocritical natures which were revealed by their reactions to His ministry.

Verses 36-50 – The story of the Pharisee and the sinner woman who anointed Jesus' feet illustrates the contrast between genuine, but simple, loving faith and scholarly, but self-righteous, religion.

Prayer Focus: Lord, help me to react to Your life and ministry with the same kind of faith and love as did the centurion and the sinner woman. Amen.

Notes:

Spiritual Journal:

Week: Eleven
Day: Tuesday
Book: Luke
Chapter: Eight
Memory Verse: Fifteen
Principle: The condition of our hearts determines what kind of results we will receive
from the Word of God.

Outline:

Verses 1-3 – These verses introduce the topic of the seed by speaking of individuals who supported Jesus' ministry with their financial substance.

Verses 4-15 – Jesus gives and explains the parable of the sower.

Verses 16-18 – Jesus explains that what is inside a person will become outwardly visible like a candle on a candle holder.   He adds that more   will be given to the one who already has something.   He is likely speaking of having inner quality which results in outward increase just as the good soil yielded an abundant harvest.

Verses 19-21 – Jesus' family illustrates the wayside soil which was fruitless.

Verses 22-25 – The disciples illustrate the thorny soil when the troubles of life rob them of their faith.

Verses 26-56 – The demoniac, the woman with the issue of blood, and Jairus all illustrate the good soil as they produce miraculous harvests while those around them demonstrate the poor soils which produce nothing.

Prayer Focus: Lord, I'm willing to be plowed and tilled in order to get the stones and thistles out of my life so that I can be good soil.   Amen.

Notes:

Spiritual Journal:

Week: Eleven

Day: Wednesday

Book: Luke

Chapter: Nine

Memory Verse: Eleven

Principle: This chapter serves as a commentary on the points of Jesus' ministry as enumerated in the memory verse: He received or accepted the people, He taught them about the Kingdom of God, and He healed them.

Outline:

Verses 1-6 – Jesus shares His ministry with His disciples.

Verses 7-9 – Questions are raised as to Jesus' identity.

Verses 10-11 – Jesus intends to retreat with His disciples; but the crowds follow Him, and He receives them.

Verses 12-17 – Jesus miraculously feeds the multitude.

Verses 18-22 – Jesus is finally able to get back to His intent in verse ten when He calls the disciples apart to discuss with them the question of His identity.

Verses 23-26 – Jesus explains that there are qualifications which must be met to be received by Him.

Verses 27-36 – The transfiguration verifies His identity.

Verses 37-62 – Various encounters illustrate Jesus' willingness to receive those who would come to Him.

a) He does not reject the disciples even though He is displeased at their lack of faith and inability to deliver the demon-possessed boy.

b) He does not reject the disciples when they begin to seek for position and rank.

c) He does not reject the minister whom the disciples want to sanction because he is not one of them.

d) He does not refuse the Samaritans, as was the custom among the Jews of His time.

e) He is willing to receive the half-hearted followers who come to Him claiming to be willing to follow Him but who have reservations in their hearts.

Prayer Focus: Lord, thank you for being willing to receive me; help me to always live in light of Your undeserved graciousness toward me. Amen.

Notes and Spiritual Journal:

Week: Eleven

Day: Thursday

Book: Luke

Chapter: Ten

Memory Verse: Sixteen

Principle: The theme of this chapter is the ministry of evangelism, but it is tempered at the end with the story of Mary, who chose the "better part" by showing her love and devotion to Jesus when her sister tried to prove herself by busily serving the Lord.

Outline:

Verses 1-16 – Jesus sent seventy witnesses out with a mandate to preach and minister.

Verses 17-24 – When they returned with their victory reports of their ministry accomplishments, He refocused their attention on their relationship with Him rather than their work for Him.

Verses 25-37 – The lawyer's question and Jesus' response with the Parable of the Good Samaritan proclaimed that the first obligation of man is to love God and that the second obligation is a simple outgrowth or manifestation of that love in showing love toward others.

Verses 38-42 – The visit to Mary and Martha's house contrasts service for service's sake and devotion which leads to service for love's sake.

Prayer Focus: Lord, You know that I want to serve and that I want to love; help me serve through love. Amen.

Notes:

Spiritual Journal:

Week: Eleven
Day: Friday
Book: Luke
Chapter: Eleven
Memory Verse: Nine

Principle: In this chapter, Jesus speaks of the divided kingdom which will fall; this thought seems to separate the chapter into two sections – the first dealing with the unity of the Kingdom of God through prayer, and the second showing the impending woes upon the kingdom of Satan which is filled with divisiveness and sabotage.

Outline:

      Verses 1-13 – Jesus teaches on prayer. One major point which He makes is often missed or misunderstood. When He taught about the person who pestered his friend until he got out of bed and gave him some bread, the petitioning should not be seen as symbolic of prayer. The verses immediately following illustrate the readiness with which God answers the prayers of His children. The point is that God does more to bless His children than even the best of human friends.

      Verses 14-26 – The accusations brought against Jesus as He was casting out devils served as a platform for Jesus to teach on the unity of the Kingdom of God.

      Verses 27-41 – Jesus described the potential for blessing afforded to His present generation.

      Verses 42-54 – The woes which they deserve are uttered against those who are unreceptive of God's Son.

Prayer Focus: Lord, I want Your blessings, not Your woes; help me to pray and live in such a way as to not miss You and Your gifts. Amen.

Notes:

Spiritual Journal:

Week: Twelve
Day: Monday
Book: Luke
Chapter: Twelve
Memory Verse: Thirty-four

Principle: Honesty to the very core of our person – the secret place of the heart – is the key to success or failure in the Kingdom of God. This chapter reveals the hypocrisy of the religious leaders, exposes the lack of in-depth soul searching of the rich fool, and explores some areas in which believers may fail to be totally honest in their inner motivations.

Outline:

    Verses 1-3 – Jesus admonished His followers to do in-depth soul searching.

    Verses 4-9 – He further admonished them to be aware of the fears and areas of respect which motivated their actions.

    Verses 10-12 – Admonition to rely upon the Holy Spirit is given.

    Verses 13-34 – The rich fool is used as a contrast against which to teach the proper heart attitude toward possessions.

    Verses 35-48 – Jesus showed how proper stewardship is a necessity for being ready for the Lord's return.

    Verses 49-53 – The Kingdom of God will become a point of importance and decision which will even bring division among family members.

    Verses 54-57 – Jesus admonished His followers to apply sincerity to discerning the signs of the time.

    Verses 58-59 – This encouragement to settle arguments as peaceably as possible is a deterrent to misinterpreting the earlier teaching about the divisions which will occur because of the gospel message; believers are not to encourage any disagreements or divisions in the name of God.

Prayer Focus: Lord, help me not to fool myself; let me be honest and crystal-clear in all my motives. Amen.

Notes:

Spiritual Journal:

Week: Twelve

Day: Tuesday

Book: Luke

Chapter: Thirteen

Memory Verse: Thirty

Principle: This chapter deals with what it takes to be admitted into or excluded from the Kingdom of God; some of the anticipated visible signs are excluded and some of the unexpected unseen indicators are brought to the forefront.

Outline:

Verses 1-5 – The individuals who brought up the topic of the tragic demise of certain contemporaries were likely trying to impose blame upon them, but Jesus deflected that blame directly to the ones who had tried to defame the others.

Verses 6-9 – The parable of the unproductive fig tree sets the stage for Jesus' teachings and actions in relationship to God's longsuffering, coupled with His ultimate sense of judgment.

Verses 10-17 – The healing of the deformed woman exposes a deadly trait which hinders entrance into the Kingdom of God – hypocrisy.

Verses 18-21 – The secret, but productive, power of the Kingdom of God is illustrated in two parables.

Verses 22-30 – Jesus admonishes His hearers to look beneath the surface to see if they really qualify for the Kingdom, since many who expect to enter in will be left outside.

Verses 31-35 – Jesus reveals His relationship to the political powers of Israel and His prophetic destiny in relationship to the city of Jerusalem when He proclaims that He will keep His schedule regardless of the political climate and the unwillingness of the people to accept His mission.

Prayer Focus: Lord, help me to get my eyes off the seen and to focus on the unseen so that I can truly know how I "rate on Your scorecard" for qualifying to inherit the Kingdom of God. Amen.

Notes:

Spiritual Journal:

Week: Twelve
Day: Wednesday
Book: Luke
Chapter: Fourteen
Memory Verse: Eleven
Principle: Jesus' teaching in this section of scripture covers several points, with a general focus on the contrast between the natural order and the Kingdom of God; the unimportant ones in the natural realm are the greatest in God's eyes, and the self-important here are rejected by God.

Outline:

Verses 1-6 – Jesus answered the scorn of the Pharisees with a question which proved them all guilty of breaking the Sabbath laws they accused Him of violating.

Verses 7-11 – Jesus taught against pride and self-importance.

Verses 12-15 – Jesus challenged prideful motives and set a standard of acceptance toward the rejected.

Verses 16-24 – The parable of the feast expands the idea of rejection to the point of recognizing that the invited guests were actually rejecting God and His Kingdom and that God would eventually reject them.

Verses 25-33 – Jesus declared that there was a cost and commitment to becoming one of His followers.

Verses 34-35 – The loss of character which disqualifies the believer is illustrated in the parable of the salt.

Prayer Focus: Lord, sometimes it is so easy to fit into the physical mold and miss spiritual reality; help me to not be caught in that trap. Amen.

Notes:

Spiritual Journal:

Week: Twelve

Day: Thursday

Book: Luke

Chapter: Fifteen

Memory Verse: Twenty-four

Principle: When Jesus was confronted by the religious Jews, who were offended that He was accepting of sinners, He taught them about the beauty of recovering lost treasures – signifying the redemption of lost humanity.

Outline:

Verses 1-2 – Contention arises among the religious leaders.

Verses 3-7 – Jesus answered with the parable of the lost sheep and the joy its recovery elicited.

Verses 8-10 – The parable of the lost coin reiterates the point.

Verses 11-32 – The parable of the lost son expands the message to include a section about a sullen brother who refused to rejoice when the lost son returned. This expansion focused on the erroneous attitude of the critics.

Prayer Focus: Lord, help me to always come running home as soon as I realize that I'm lost and to never discourage or criticize any lost one who is trying to make his way back home. Amen.

Notes:

Spiritual Journal:

Week: Twelve
Day: Friday
Book: Luke
Chapter: Sixteen
Memory Verse: Seventeen
Principle: Jesus gave several parables and teachings which all focus on the principle that monetary wealth cannot be substituted for spiritual prosperity.
Outline:

Verses 1-8 – The parable of the unjust steward is very often misunderstood because it says that the lord commended his steward for the deed and then adds that the children of this generation are wiser than the children of light. It must be remembered that Jesus did not commend the steward; in fact, Jesus continued to label the man as being unjust. It must also be remembered that Jesus did not commend the children of this generation; He simply used them as a standard of comparison to show His lack of commendation to the children of light. It seems, rather, that Jesus is saying that the members of His Kingdom are too slothful in taking advantage of the opportunities afforded us.

Verses 9-13 – In the explanation following the parable, Jesus emphasized that He was not advocating reliance upon monetary wealth when He told the disciples to use money to make friends to turn to when it failed (something which believers are not expected to do). He also told them that their friends with money were to receive them into everlasting habitations (something which only God can do). He concluded that serving mammon precludes serving God and vice versa.

Verses 14-18 – Jesus zeros in on the covetousness of the hearts of the Pharisees and demonstrates to them that they have tried to negate the laws of God which are indestructible.

Verses 19-31 – The story of Lazarus and the rich man illustrates the foolishness of trusting in riches and the reward of serving God.

Prayer Focus: Lord, help me to recognize Your true riches. Amen.
Notes:

Spiritual Journal:

Week: Thirteen
Day: Monday
Book: Luke
Chapter: Seventeen
Memory Verse: Six
Principle: This chapter seems to be woven around the thought of the qualities of true faith. When the disciples ask to have their faith increased, Jesus answers with a statement that shows that they don't need to have their faith increased, but rather to have the first installment of true faith: if they had any faith at all – even as much as a mustard seed – they would already be doing great feats. Other passages in the section describe a heart attitude out of which faith can emerge: forgiveness, servitude, thankfulness, internalizing the Kingdom of God, and anticipation.
Outline:
> Verses 1-4 – Jesus deals with the problems of wrongdoing: causing offense and taking offense.
>
> Verses 5-6 – Jesus makes the disciples aware that they are truly lacking in genuine faith.
>
> Verses 7-10 – The heart of a servant is illustrated.
>
> Verses 11-19 – Thankfulness characterized the difference between the one leper who was said to have faith and the other nine.
>
> Verses 20-25 – The Kingdom of God is manifest inside rather than outside the person of true faith.
>
> Verses 26-37 – The expectant heart makes all the difference in the world for the individual with true faith as he awaits the coming of the Son of Man.

Prayer Focus: Lord, I want to be a man who demonstrates true faith, not just one who produces demonstrations of faith. Amen.
Notes:

Spiritual Journal:

Week: Thirteen
Day: Tuesday
Book: Luke
Chapter: Eighteen
Memory Verse: Seventeen
Principle: This chapter further expands the idea of the true heart attitude of a person of genuine faith.

Outline:

Verses 1-8 – The story of the unjust judge who eventually avenged the widow is often misinterpreted to be a teaching on persistent prayer. When this interpretation is given, the judge is seen as representing God. In actuality, the story was told to illustrate that God (in contrast to the unjust judge) quickly responds to people of true faith. The story ends with a summary statement which clearly ties it to the theme of this section, "When the Son of Man comes, will He find faith on the earth?"

Verses 9-14 – Jesus exposed the futility of trusting in one's own goodness.

Verses 15-17 – Child-like faith is declared as a prerequisite for entering the Kingdom of God.

Verses 18-30 – The detriment of a wrong heart attitude toward physical prosperity is exposed.

Verses 31-34 – The lack of spiritual perception by even the disciples is illustrated in their inability to comprehend Jesus' teachings about His coming Passion.

Verses 35-43 – A blind beggar with an eager heart and a desperate need demonstrates what a man of real faith is.

Prayer Focus: Lord, again, I pray that I might have genuine faith that pleases You, not the human substitute or a reasonable facsimile thereof. Amen.

Notes:

Spiritual Journal:

Week: Thirteen
Day: Wednesday
Book: Luke
Chapter: Nineteen
Memory Verse: Forty
Principle: There is an underlying theme which unifies the seemingly unrelated sections of this chapter: stewardship. Whether of money, position, or praise – stewardship is demanded in every arena of life.
Outline:
        Verses 1-8 – Zacchaeus spontaneously began to think and talk stewardship immediately upon his conversion.
        Verses 9-27 – In His parable of the talents, Jesus demonstrated that each man's ultimate destiny hinges on his stewardship.
        Verses 28-40 – The idea of having a responsibility to praise God – or actually to be a steward over praise which is due to Him – is illustrated in the story of the Triumphal Entry. An interesting theme of stewardship in relation to the donkey accents this section.
        Verses 41-48 – The people of the city of Jerusalem and the religious leaders proved to have been unfaithful stewards of the revelation and visitation of God and of the spiritual position which had been given to them.
Prayer Focus: Lord, I want to be seen as a worthy and trusted steward. Amen.
Notes:

Spiritual Journal:

Week: Thirteen

Day: Thursday

Book: Luke

Chapter: Twenty

Memory Verse: Twenty-five

Principle: During His visit to the Temple, Jesus is accosted by representatives from every leading branch of Judaism as they try to trick Him; but truth always wins out, demonstrating the point that God will vindicate His own.

Outline:

Verses 1-26 – The chief priests and scribes are silenced.

a) Their challenge concerning Jesus' authority is overruled.

b) They cannot answer Jesus' parable about them.

c) Their trick question on taxes brings them – rather than Jesus – under scrutiny.

Verses 27-38 – The Sadducees find that their question to Jesus shows their own stupidity rather than tricking Jesus.

Verses 39-47 – Not only are Jesus' opponents silenced, they are also brought under scrutiny by their followers.

Prayer Focus: Lord, I ask You to examine my heart and see if I have any of the evil of these pious critics of Yours in me.   Amen.

Notes:

\

Spiritual Journal:

Week: Thirteen
Day: Friday
Book: Luke
Chapter: Twenty-one
Memory Verse: Thirty-six

Principle: This chapter echoes Amos 3:7 in that it assures us that God will not do anything unless He first reveals it to His servants the prophets; the Day of the Lord should not catch any believer by surprise since a multitude of signs are outlined for us to observe.

Outline:

Verses 1-4 – The story of the widow's mite serves as a transition from the previous topic, which concludes with the accusation that the religious leaders devour widows. The new topic which begins with the notation that the Temple which the widow is supporting is adorned with costly stones and gifts. This story is also anchored into the former discussion on stewardship in that the widow was acting in genuine stewardship even though the ornate Temple was obviously not in need of her tiny offering.

Verses 5-28 – Jesus offers signs which foretell the Day of the Lord.

a) False Christs will come

b) War

c) Natural catastrophes

d) Persecution

e) Jerusalem will be attacked

f) Cosmic upheaval

Verses 29-36 – The hearers are warned to observe these signs and respond as they see them being fulfilled. It is interesting that Jesus mentions eating and drinking and taking care of daily responsibilities as the prime causes for people who will fail to observe the signs of the times.

Verses 37-38 – These last verses inform us that Jesus had a large audience up to the very end of His ministry. It is interesting that these followers will fail to come to His defense when He is taken to trial within the week. They were hearers but not responders – exactly the problem Jesus warns us about in relation to the coming of the Day of the Lord.

Prayer Focus: Lord, James 1:23 admonishes us concerning the determinate difference between being a hearer of the Word and being a doer of it – help me not to hear only, but also to act. Amen.

Notes and Spiritual Journal:

Week: Fourteen
Day: Monday
Book: Luke
Chapter: Twenty-two
Memory Verse: Forty-two

Principle: Today's chapter contains the stories of the Last Supper, Christ's agony in the garden, the arrest, and the trial of Jesus. Within this context, one simple theme seems to reappear: the deceptiveness of the human heart, as revealed in Judas' betrayal of the Lord, Peter's denial of Him, the disciples' spending their last meal with Jesus by arguing among themselves about their own importance, their sleeping through His greatest trial, and Jesus' own struggle with submission to the Father's will.

Outline:

Verses 1-6 – Judas strikes a deal with the chief priests and scribes.

Verses 7-20 – Jesus serves the Last Supper and illustrates His covenant commitment to the disciples without respect to the deceptiveness of their hearts which is to be revealed as the chapter unfolds.

Verses 21-34 – The secrets of the disciples' hearts are revealed as they are challenged with the fact that one of them is a betrayer, they begin to argue about position, and Peter displays questionable loyalty.

Verses 35-38 – Jesus warns the disciples to prepare for their upcoming mission.

Verses 39-46 – The agony in the garden shows the disciples' inability to associate with the struggle Jesus Himself had to endure in coming to the place of total submission to the will of the Father.

Verses 47-53 – The story of the arrest of Jesus accentuates the idea of the heart attitudes when Jesus heals the ear of one member of the arresting party. No malice whatever was found in His heart.

Verses 54-71 – The trial of Jesus demonstrates the true heart attitude of Peter as he stood away from the Lord and as he denied Him, but it also shows the reversal of his heart as he wept bitterly and repented. Jesus' blameless heart is revealed through His interrogation and accusation.

Prayer Focus: Lord, don't let my heart deceive me, but let my spirit serve as the candle of the Lord searching my innermost being. Amen.

Notes and Spiritual Journal:

Week: Fourteen
Day: Tuesday
Book: Luke
Chapter: Twenty-three
Memory Verse: Four

Principle: Today's memory verse says it all – there was no fault in Jesus. Just as this chapter proves it over and over, living our lives in dependence upon Him will repeatedly prove that no fault can ever be found in Him.

Outline:

Verses 1-5 – Pilate finds no fault in Him.

Verses 6-15 – Herod finds no fault in Jesus.

Verses 16-26 – Pilate reiterates his evaluation that Jesus is faultless.

Verses 27-31 – Jesus' response to the women showed that He carried no malice.

Verses 32-43 – Even the thief who was being crucified with the Lord confirmed His faultlessness.

Verses 44-49 – The executioner also established the Lord's righteousness.

Verses 50-56 – The burial of the body was undertaken by Joseph, who was called "a good man and just." Perhaps this evaluation was a deliberate choice of words to continue the theme.

Prayer Focus: Lord, may I also be evaluated as a man in whom no fault can be found. Amen.

Notes:

Spiritual Journal:

Week: Fourteen
Day: Wednesday
Book: Luke
Chapter: Twenty-four
Memory Verse: Twenty-five
Principle: The greatest victory story of all history is riddled with disbelief and questions.
Outline:

        Verses 1-7 – The women at the tomb are perplexed.

        Verses 8-12 – The disciples received the testimony of the resurrection as idle words.

        Verses 13-35 – The disciples on the road to Emmaus questioned and wondered.

        Verses 36-45 – The disciples were troubled and doubting at the appearance of the risen Lord.

        Verses 46-53 – After the Great Commission, a blessing, and the Ascension, the disciples were able to overcome their doubts and questions.

Prayer Focus: Lord, I believe; help my unbelief.   Amen.
Notes:

Spiritual Journal:

Week: Fourteen
Day: Thursday
Book: John
Chapter: One
Memory Verse: Fourteen
Principle: The focus of this chapter – and, indeed, the whole book of John – is summed up in today's memory verse: Jesus is God incarnate among us.
Outline:
Verses 1-14 – Two great theological themes – Word and Light – are introduced. These concepts show Jesus as the source of life:
a) Theologically, everything had its origin in the creative Word of God when God spoke the worlds into existence.
b) Biologically, all life is dependent upon light for existence.
Verses 15-28 – The preeminence of Jesus is demonstrated over the law and prophets, and especially over John the Baptist, in that He is the source of life, truth, and grace.
Verses 29-34 – Two new themes – the Lamb of God and the Son of God – are introduced.
Verses 35-51 – As Jesus began to gather His disciples, He consistently demonstrated that He is uniquely superior to any individual they have ever encountered.
Prayer Focus: Lord, help me to have my spiritual eyes open to see You in the fullness of who You really are.   Amen.
Notes:

Spiritual Journal:

Week: Fourteen
Day: Friday
Book: John
Chapter: Two
Memory Verse: Eleven
Principle: One of the major focuses of the book of John is introduced in this chapter: signs or miracles were done in order to help people believe that Jesus is the Son of God.

Outline:

Verses 1-11 – The miracle of changing the water into wine had some symbolic significance in that the water came from the pots of purification used within the Jewish rituals. When that water became wine (which is symbolic of the Holy Spirit), the ideas of the new birth and of the emergence of the Christian faith are illustrated. However, there is also a practical principle being set forth: Jesus' performance of miracles was a sign to the observers that He is the Son of God.

Verses 12-17 – The story of the cleansing of the Temple bears a new significance in the book of John which is not stressed in the other gospels. Here, the emphasis is not on the Temple itself as much as on Jesus' relationship to the Temple that it is His Father's house, emphasizes the revelation that Jesus is the Son of God.

Verses 18-22 – Here, very early in the book, John introduces the concept that the most significant sign of Jesus' divinity will be His resurrection.

Verses 23-25 – John explains that even though the signs did serve their purpose of causing people to believe in Jesus, He was looking for more than superficial acceptance based on His ability to perform miracles; He was looking for something on the inside of those who followed Him.

Prayer Focus: Lord, I believe in You and Your miracles, but I also believe that You are searching my heart; may You find only what You are desiring inside it. Amen.

Notes:

Spiritual Journal:

Week: Fifteen
Day: Monday
Book: John
Chapter: Three
Memory Verse: Sixteen
Principle: This chapter uses two characters to express the same truth – our acceptance or rejection of Christ is the determining factor between eternal life and eternal judgment.
Outline:

Verses 1-8 – Jesus explained to Nicodemus that we must have a new birth in our spiritual man in order to enter God's Kingdom.

Verses 9-13 – Jesus began to reveal to Nicodemus (even though he was a religious leader) the spiritual reality of life.

Verses 14-21 – Jesus used the story of Moses and the brass serpent to illustrate the truth that man can only be saved by accepting the cure which God has provided in the crucified Christ.

Verses 22-36 – John the Baptist reaffirmed the same principle, that acceptance or rejection of Christ is the deciding factor between everlasting life and the wrath of God.

a) John affirmed that he was not the Christ.

b) He preached that Jesus was the one sent from God.

c) He concluded that Jesus, as God's Son, is the only way to come to God.

Prayer Focus: Lord, help me to genuinely believe upon You so that I might have Your everlasting life.   Amen.
Notes:

Spiritual Journal:

Week: Fifteen

Day: Tuesday

Book: John

Chapter: Four

Memory Verse: Twenty-four

Principle: This chapter seems to build on the theme of the previous chapter by showing how some unlikely individuals believed on Christ and received life.

Outline:

Verses 1-26 – The woman at the well of Samaria

a) Jesus asked her for water and offered her living water.

b) She marveled at His revelation concerning her past and decided that He must be a prophet.

c) When He began to explain the spiritual principles of the Kingdom of God, she began to suspect that He was the Messiah – a truth which He confirmed.

Verses 27-42 – The Samaritans

a) The Samaritans were outcasts in the eyes of the Jews; however, the woman's testimony was enough to convince them to come to hear and receive the Messiah she had found.

b) Jesus amazed His disciples by telling them that, in ministering to these spiritually hungry people, He was satisfied spiritually in a way that overruled His physical need for food.

Verses 43-54 – The nobleman's son in Cana was healed.

a) The father was desperate and refused to be moved from his faith.

b) His belief on Jesus was rewarded when his son received his physical life.

Prayer Focus: Lord, I want to worship You in spirit and in truth; help me to never stop short of the true spiritual faith.   Amen.

Notes:

Spiritual Journal:

Week: Fifteen
Day: Wednesday
Book: John
Chapter: Five
Memory Verse: Twenty-four
Principle: This chapter continues the theme of the previous two chapters by illustrating the negative side of the equation: those who refused to believe.
Outline:
Verses 1-14 – Jesus performed a great miracle by healing a man who had been crippled for thirty-eight years, but, rather than rejoicing at the miracle, the religious leaders responded in criticism because Jesus had violated their Sabbath laws.
Verses 15-18 – They added a second reason for their hatred of Jesus when He began to share about His relationship with God.
Verses 19-30 – Jesus taught them concerning His pivotal role in receiving the resurrection to eternal life.
Verses 31-47 – Jesus warned them that they were rejecting four witnesses to His person:
a) John the Baptist
b) The miracles of Jesus
c) The Father Himself
d) The Old Testament
Prayer Focus: Lord, there is so much evidence before us that You truly are the Lord of the universe; help me to allow You to be Lord of my own little universe.   Amen.
Notes:

Spiritual Journal:

Week: Fifteen

Day: Thursday

Book: John

Chapter: Six

Memory Verse: Fifty-one

Principle: In most cultures, the terminology of bread is used to speak of life and life-sustaining qualities; when Jesus used this terminology to speak of Himself, He affirmed the theme of John that Jesus is the life.

Outline:

Verses 1-14 – Jesus miraculously fed a multitude of more than five thousand.

Verses 15-26 – Jesus miraculously walked on the sea but commented that the people had not caught the meaning of the miracle bread.

Verses 27-59 – Jesus taught them the meaning of the bread – that He Himself was the bread from God that gave eternal life.

Verses 60-71 – This teaching drew the dividing line between those who would stay with Him and those who would abandon Him.

Prayer Focus: Lord, You are the Bread of Life, and I know that I will starve spiritually without You; help me to have a healthy spiritual appetite and the proper spiritual diet. Amen.

Notes:

Spiritual Journal:

Week: Fifteen
Day: Friday
Book: John
Chapter: Seven
Memory Verse: Forty-six
Principle: The previous chapter ended with the proclamation, "You have the words of life." But this chapter illustrates how unbelief can deafen the ears from hearing those living words.
Outline:
Verses 1-9 – Even Jesus' own brothers did not believe in Him and tried to trick Him into falling into a trap.
Verses 10-18 – The people could tell that Jesus' words were not those from formal education, but they refused to believe that they were the Word of God.
Verses 19-52 – Although various objections were raised against Him, Jesus was not arrested because it was not yet His appointed time.
a) Is He going to the Greeks?
b) How can anyone know where the Messiah is from?
c) Has a prophet ever come from Galilee?
d) Have any of the leaders ever believed on Him?
Prayer Focus: Lord, help me to get beyond the petty questions and arguments of men and focus on Your words of life. Amen.
Notes:

Spiritual Journal:

Week: Sixteen
Day: Monday
Book: John
Chapter: Eight
Memory Verse: Thirty-six
Principle: The underlying theme of this section can be summed up in the words of verse 47, "He that is of God heareth God's words: ye therefore hear them not, because ye are not of God."
Outline:
        Verses 1-12 – When the accusers in this story of the woman caught in adultery slipped away as Jesus wrote in the sand, it illustrated the principle that those who are not of God will not hear His words.

        Verses 13-30 – Jesus' discussion with the Pharisees proved that they not only didn't know Him but that they didn't even know God.

        Verses 31-59 – The Pharisees claimed their heritage as Abraham's descendants; yet, Jesus proved their unworthiness as Abraham's true seed.
            a) They were not free.
            b) They didn't do the works of Abraham.
            c) They could not understand the truth.
            d) They did not rejoice in seeing the coming of the Messiah.
Prayer Focus: Lord, I want to hear Your words and have Your life; help me not to slip away as the woman's accusers did when You write on the sand of my heart. Amen.
Notes:

Spiritual Journal:

Week: Sixteen
Day: Tuesday
Book: John
Chapter: Nine
Memory Verse: Thirty-nine
Principle: A theme that runs throughout the book of John is the "Light of the World" and that man is given the opportunity and option to believe on Him or to reject His light. In this section, the reactions of the Pharisees to the healing of the blind man illustrated that some choose to remain in darkness rather than to accept the Light.
Outline:
Verses 1-5 – The man's blindness was not from sin (remember this point when you read verse thirty-four).
Verses 6-12 – The man was healed.
Verses 13-34 – The Pharisees examined the man.
a) They questioned that he was the same man and that a miracle had actually occurred.
b) They suggested that God be praised but that Jesus not be mentioned in the testimony.
c) Rather than accept the obvious, they began to accuse the man who had been blind.
Verses 35-39 – The man acknowledged Jesus.
Verses 40-41 – Jesus explained that the Pharisees were the truly blind ones in this story.
Prayer Focus: Lord, I understand that men love darkness because their deeds are evil; help me to love Your light and desire to walk in it. Amen.
Notes:

Spiritual Journal:

Week: Sixteen
Day: Wednesday
Book: John
Chapter: Ten
Memory Verse: Fourteen
Principle: The thesis of this section is that true sheep know the true Shepherd and ones who are not sheep will reject Him.
Outline:
Verses 1-18 – The Shepherd's care for the sheep:
a) He knows them and is known by them.
b) He protects them from enemies.
c) Unlike a hireling, He will give His life for them.
d) He will bring other sheep into the fold.
Verses 19-21 – There was disagreement among the people because some were sheep and some were not.
Verses 22-30 – The feast of Hanukkah when the Jews celebrated their deliverance from the Greeks became the backdrop for the question of whether Jesus was the Messiah.
Verses 31-39 – When the Jews tried to stone Jesus for blasphemy because He stated His relationship to God, He challenged them with Old Testament scriptures which they were accustomed to misinterpreting.
Verses 40-42 – Many outside Jerusalem believed on Jesus – they were sheep!
Prayer Focus: Lord, I find that it is just too easy to listen to the voice of others and to follow them; help me to be a true sheep who pays attention to You alone. Amen.
Notes:

Spiritual Journal:

Week: Sixteen
Day: Thursday
Book: John
Chapter: Eleven
Memory Verse: Twenty-five
Principle: The raising of Lazarus from the dead teaches many lessons. One principle of prayer demonstrated here is that Jesus' private prayer allowed Him to perform a great miracle with only a short public prayer. A second lesson on faith is illustrated in that what looked like a failure when Jesus did not come to heal Lazarus was actually God's platform for a much greater miracle. Another lesson on compassion is found in the illustration of Jesus' love for Lazarus and his sisters. There is also an explanation of the glory of God in that there is a shift at this point from the use of the term "glory" to refer to miracles to a new meaning having to do with the death and resurrection. Additionally, there is a promise of eternal life when Jesus proclaimed Himself to be the Resurrection and the Life. There is also a foreshadowing of the resurrection of Jesus in that this miracle precipitated the final plot against Jesus' life.
Outline:
Verses 1-6 – Lazarus' death
Verses 7-37 – The question of Jesus' authority over death and dying
Verses 38-44 – The raising of Lazarus
Verses 45-57 – The plot to kill Jesus
Prayer Focus: Lord, as a human, I tend to avoid the topic of death and dying until it confronts me face to face; today, I pray that I'll learn the victorious stance I can take toward this enemy in that You, the Resurrection and Life, are inside of me. Amen.
Notes:

Spiritual Journal:

Week: Sixteen
Day: Friday
Book: John
Chapter: Twelve
Memory Verse: Thirty-two
Principle: Perhaps verse sixteen expresses one thought which sums up the message of this
        chapter: if even the disciples could not understand who Jesus was, certainly the
        Jews whose hearts were hardened would reject Him.
Outline:
        Verses 1-8 – Mary anointed Jesus' feet, but Judas objected that such an
           extravagant gift be expended on Jesus.
        Verses 9-11 – The guests who attended the celebration feast were more interested
           in Lazarus than in Jesus, and some plotted to kill him in order to hide the
           evidence of Jesus' miracle.
        Verses 12-22 – These verses show the magnetism that caused "the world to go
           after" Jesus even though they had no revelation of who He was.
        Verses 23-27 – Jesus predicted His death.
        Verses 28-30 – The Father reassured Him that death would be followed by
           glorification.
        Verses 31-36 – The people grappled with their preconceived concepts of the
           Messiah.
        Verses 37-41 – John explained the prophetic background to the people's inability
           to receive Christ.
        Verses 42-43 – Some leaders elected to do the popular thing rather than to stand
           up for their belief in Christ.
        Verses 44-50 – John reintroduced the themes of Light and Life which run
           throughout the book.
Prayer Focus: Lord, I don't want to ever love the praises of man more than the praises of
        God. Amen.
Notes:

Spiritual Journal:

Week: Seventeen
Day: Monday
Book: John
Chapter: Thirteen
Memory Verse: Thirty-five
Principle: The lesson Jesus taught by washing the disciples' feet (the job of the lowest servant) illustrated the kind of self-abasing love He expects of His disciples.
Outline:
>   Verses 1-17 – Jesus washed the disciples' feet and explained that they should also live as servants rather than as masters.
>
>   Verses 18-30 – Jesus indicated His betrayer by sharing a sop with him – a symbol of close fellowship or brotherhood.
>
>   Verses 31-35 – Jesus predicted that He would depart but left the disciples with one last command – to love one another.
>
>   Verses 36-38 – Peter's promise to defend the Lord, countered by Jesus' response that, instead, he would deny Him, proved that men not only do not recognize God, they may not even know themselves.

Prayer Focus: Lord, the very thought of becoming a washer of others' feet stirs up a reaction inside me; help me to have Your heart so that I desire to be a servant. Amen.

Notes:

Spiritual Journal:

Week: Seventeen
Day: Tuesday
Book: John
Chapter: Fourteen
Memory Verse: Twenty-one
Principle: This chapter, along with the following two and the prayer in chapter seventeen, is the final discourse of Jesus in which He prepares the disciples for life after His departure.
Outline:
 Verses 1-6 – Jesus used the Jewish marriage tradition as an illustration that He would come back for His Bride, the church.
 Verses 7-11 – Jesus explained His relationship with the Father.
 Verses 12-14 – Jesus explained the conditions for receiving answers to prayer.
 Verses 15-18 – Jesus gave the promise of the coming of the Holy Spirit.
 Verses 19-24 – Jesus related loving Him to keeping His commands.
 Verses 25-29 – Jesus promised peace and the Holy Spirit.
 Verses 30-31 – Jesus contrasted His relationship with the Father against His confrontation with the enemy.
Prayer Focus: Lord, today I pray a simple line from a sincere song of worship: "Come, Holy Spirit." Amen.
Notes:

Spiritual Journal:

Week: Seventeen
Day: Wednesday
Book: John
Chapter: Fifteen
Memory Verse: Five
Principle: There is no neutral position in relationship to Jesus – either you are abiding in Him or not; either you love Him and the Father or you hate Him and the Father.
Outline:
>   Verses 1-8 – Jesus taught a parable showing the necessity of abiding in Him.
>   Verses 9-17 – Love evidenced by keeping the commandments is the key to abiding in Christ and being filled with His joy.
>   Verses 18-25 – Those who are not part of the vine and are not abiding in love are full of hate toward God and His followers.
>   Verses 26-27 – There will be two witnesses concerning Christ: the Holy Spirit and His followers.

Prayer Focus: Lord, my life source is dependent upon my abiding in You; help me to stay vitally attached. Amen.
Notes:

Spiritual Journal:

Week: Seventeen

Day: Thursday

Book: John

Chapter: Sixteen

Memory Verse: Seven

Principle: As is only natural, the disciples did not want Jesus to be taken from them; but Jesus listed a number of advantages which were in store for them: the coming of the Holy Spirit, the joy of the resurrection, a fuller revelation of Christ's deity, a new source of answered prayer, and a new level of overcoming authority.

Outline:

        Verses 1-6 – Jesus forewarned the disciples of coming troubles as a background for the rest of His teaching concerning the coming promise and provision.

        Verses 7-15 – Jesus promised the coming of the Spirit of truth, who would reveal all things of the Father to the followers of Christ.

        Verses 16-24 – Jesus spoke of His death and resurrection in a parable and gave a new promise of answered prayer.

        Verses 25-30 – Jesus revealed the mystery that He was to go to the Father.

        Verses 31-33 – Jesus ended His teaching with a note of triumph.

Prayer Focus: Lord, I invite the Holy Spirit to do His work of convicting today, and I yield myself to His correction.   Amen.

Notes:

Spiritual Journal:

Week: Seventeen

Day: Friday

Book: John

Chapter: Seventeen

Memory Verse: Fifteen

Principle: Jesus ended His last ministry to His disciples by praying for them that they would have a new relationship with the Father to protect and guide them in the new situations they would face.

Outline:

Verses 1-5 – Jesus prayed to be returned to His divine glory through the resurrection.

Verses 6-8 – Jesus established that what He had done in and for the disciples was through the power of the Father.

Verses 9-15 – Jesus prayed for the preservation of His disciples.

Verses 16-19 – Jesus prayed for their sanctification.

Verses 20-23 – He prayed for unity.

Verses 24-26 – He prayed for them to have a revelation of the Father and the Son.

Prayer Focus: Lord, You prayed that Your disciples would be one; help me not to be a divider to undo the unity You have begun.   Amen.

Notes:

Spiritual Journal:

Week: Eighteen
Day: Monday
Book: John
Chapter: Eighteen
Memory Verse: Thirty-seven
Principle: The willing sacrifice of Jesus is twice openly admitted. "I am He" is dramatically contrasted with Peter's repeated denial.
Outline:

> Verses 1-11 – Even as Jesus was betrayed by Judas and arrested, He continued His mission of compassion by healing the man whose ear was cut off.
>
> Verses 12-27 – While Jesus was being tried before Annas and Ciaphas, the high priests, Peter was on trial before the servants in the courtyard.
>
> Verses 28-38 – Pilate, the Roman governor, found no reason to try or execute Jesus.
>
> Verses 39-40 – The mob cried out for Jesus' execution.

Prayer Focus: Lord, help me to always have the courage to admit – and even proclaim – that I am Your disciple.   Amen.
Notes:

Spiritual Journal:

Week: Eighteen

Day: Tuesday

Book: John

Chapter: Nineteen

Memory Verse: Nineteen

Principle: The repeated reference to the Preparation Day indicates that Jesus is the Lamb which was symbolized in the Passover of the Old Testament.

Outline:

Verses 1-16 – The trial before Pilate determined that there was no fault in Jesus, just as the Passover lamb had to be spotless.

Verses 17-22 – Jesus was proclaimed King of the Jews in all the languages in popular use at the time.

Verses 23-24 – Every detail of His death was prophetic – even to the dividing of His garments.

Verses 25-30 – Jesus' humanity was displayed until His very moment of death in His love for His mother and His physical thirst.

Verses 31-37 – Like the Passover lamb, no bone was broken; however, His heart was pierced, verifying that He was truly dead.

Verses 38-42 – Two Jewish leaders who had been secret disciples came forward to secure His body for burial.

Prayer Focus: Lord, give me each day a fresh vision of the sacrifice You made for me. Amen.

Notes:

Spiritual Journal:

Week: Eighteen
Day: Wednesday
Book: John
Chapter: Twenty
Memory Verse: Twenty-nine
Principle: In this chapter, we see several encounters with the risen Lord in which His disciples could not believe that He had actually been raised from the dead; verse nine explains that they did not yet know, or understand, the scriptures concerning His resurrection. We, too, sometimes fall into that category of having spiritual truths right before our eyes but failing to see them.

Outline:

Verses 1-10 – Mary discovered the empty tomb and told Peter and the other disciple (John) who came and saw that the body was no longer in the grave.   They believed that He had been removed but did not yet know that He had been raised.

Verses 11-18 – Jesus revealed Himself to Mary.

Verses 19-23 – Jesus revealed Himself to the disciples on the evening of the resurrection day.

Verses 24-29 – A week later, Jesus revealed Himself to Thomas.

Verses 30-31 – John recorded that his report was written so that those who have not personally seen the risen Lord could believe on Him through the written word.

Prayer Focus: Lord, help me to believe even when I have not seen.   Amen.
Notes:

Spiritual Journal:

Week: Eighteen
Day: Thursday
Book: John
Chapter: Twenty-one
Memory Verse: Seventeen
Principle: Jesus' revelation to His disciples on the shore of the Sea of Galilee called them
    to a fresh commitment to love, follow, and serve Him.
Outline:
> Verses 1-14 – In the miraculous catch of fish, the disciples realized that this was
> the same Jesus who had originally called them after another supernatural
> catch of fish.
>
> Verses 15-17 – Jesus called Peter, the fisherman, to become a shepherd because
> of his love for the Lord. It is interesting that Jesus demanded *agape* (the
> supreme form of love) yet Peter admitted that he could only offer *philia* (a
> human quality of love).
>
> Verses 18-23 – The last request that Jesus left with His disciples was the same as
> the first one He issued to them: "Follow Me."
>
> Verses 24-25 – John concluded his text with a repetition of his purpose that the
> testimony it contains would engender faith inside the readers.

Prayer Focus: Lord, help me to learn how to move into that ultimate level of love which
    You require. Amen.
Notes:

Spiritual Journal:

Week: Eighteen
Day: Friday
Book: Acts
Chapter: One
Memory Verse: Eight
Principle: This chapter deals with the immediate reaction of the disciples to their new
role of advancing the church: hesitantly followed by physical preparation in anticipation
       of spiritual equipping.
Outline:
       Verses 1-3 – Luke's introduction connects the story he is about to tell about the
           church with the previous account he has given about the life of Jesus.
       Verses 4-8 – Jesus renewed His promise of the coming of the Holy Spirit and His
           commission to use the power of the Spirit to evangelize the world.
       Verses 9-11 – The angels climax the ascension with the reminder that Jesus will
           return again.
       Verses 12-26 – The followers of Jesus gathered in the Upper Room and elected a
           replacement for Judas.
Prayer Focus: Lord, after having heard Your promise of the empowering of the Holy
       Spirit and Your commission to go into all the world, help me to never be guilty, as
       were the disciples, of "standing here."   Amen.
Notes:

Spiritual Journal:

Week: Nineteen
Day: Monday
Book: Acts
Chapter: Two
Memory Verse: Seventeen
Principle: The power of the Holy Spirit enabled the disciples not only to speak supernaturally in other tongues, but also to speak persuasively in their own tongue.
Outline:

Verses 1-4 – The disciples were filled with the Holy Spirit as they tarried in one place with one accord.

Verses 5-13 – Their supernatural languages drew the attention of men from all parts of the ancient world.

Verses 14-36 – Peter spoke an anointed message which showed the prophetic background of the present experience and the life and death of Jesus.

Verses 37-39 – The crowd responded to Peter's message, which not only placed guilt on them but also placed a promise of salvation before them.

Verses 40-47 – With three thousand converts on the first day and additional daily growth, the church organized and established itself in Jerusalem.

Prayer Focus: Lord, grant me the effectiveness of a Spirit-anointed life and ministry. Amen.

Notes:

Spiritual Journal:

Week: Nineteen
Day: Tuesday
Book: Acts
Chapter: Three
Memory Verse: Twenty-six
Principle: A pattern for ministry known today as "power evangelism" is illustrated here when Peter and John ministered healing followed by preaching of the gospel of salvation.
Outline:
Verses 1-9 – The healing of the lame beggar drew a crowd and caught the attention of the people.
Verses 10-25 – Peter's sermon bore many similarities to his message on Pentecost in that it emphasized the prophetic background to the life and death of Jesus and placed the guilt for His death squarely upon the hearers.
Verse 26 – Peter proclaimed the promise of salvation through the resurrection of Jesus.
Prayer Focus: Lord, I claim Your promise that You will work with me and establish miraculous signs to validate my ministry. Amen.
Notes:

Spiritual Journal:

Week: Nineteen
Day: Wednesday
Book: Acts
Chapter: Four
Memory Verse: Twenty
Principle: The scriptures proclaim that all who live godly in Christ Jesus will suffer persecution; but it is also promised that those who are willing to pay the sacrificial cost will receive a victorious deliverance.
Outline:

Verses 1-4 – The healing of the lame man produced two results: five thousand converts and the ire of the religious leaders.

Verses 5-22 – The astounding nature of the miracle and the incredible boldness of the disciples left the religious council powerless except to issue threats against the apostles if they continued to preach in Jesus' name.

Verses 23-31 – Rather than backing down, the apostles prayed for continued boldness and miraculous confirmation of their ministry.

Verses 32-37 – A communal love and spirit of sharing characterized the early church.

Prayer Focus: Lord, give me the same determination to live and speak for You which we see recorded in these early fathers of the faith. Amen.
Notes:

Spiritual Journal:

Week: Nineteen
Day: Thursday
Book: Acts
Chapter: Five
Memory Verse: Twenty-nine
Principle: In the introductory verses of this book, Luke showed that the church is a continuation of the ministry of Jesus; later, at Paul's conversion. we will see that Jesus considered persecution against the church to be against Himself; this chapter also confirms that sins against the church are truly sins against God.
Outline:
    Verses 1-11 – When Ananias and Sapphira lied to the church leadership, it was seen as a lie to the Holy Ghost.
    Verses 12-21 – The miraculous power evangelism of the apostles landed them in jail again, but an angel of God supernaturally opened their prison door.
    Verses 22-33 – The trial affirms the council's understanding that the ministry of the apostles placed the blame for Jesus' death upon the Jewish people and the apostles' determination to continue their divinely commissioned assignment.
    Verses 34-40 – Gamaliel evaluated the situation correctly: fighting against the church would be fighting against God Himself.
    Verses 41-42 – The church continued to live and increase in spite of – or maybe with the encouragement of – the council's persecution.
Prayer Focus: Lord, if indeed my ministry is actually an extension of Your ministry, help me to genuinely minister in Your ability and character. Amen.
Notes:

Spiritual Journal:

Week: Nineteen
Day: Friday
Book: Acts
Chapter: Six
Memory Verse: Four
Principle: Two seemingly diverse stories present the same truth: whether trouble arises
    within the church or opposition arises from outside, the men who are graced by
    God and filled with His Spirit will become apparent and rise to the occasion.
Outline:
    Verses 1-7 – The internal problem between two cultural groups within the church
        was easily settled when men full of faith and the Holy Ghost began to
        oversee the issues.
    Verses 8-15 – Stephen's divinely anointed wisdom and miracle ministry drew the
        opposition of the Jewish council. They determined to prosecute him even
        if they had to hire men to lie against him. In all this, Stephen's godly
        character showed through and was obvious to the council.
Prayer Focus: Lord, let me be one who is obviously full of Your Spirit in every adversity.
    Amen.
Notes:

Spiritual Journal:

Week: Twenty
Day: Monday
Book: Acts
Chapter: Seven
Memory Verse: Fifty-five
Principle: The history of Israel was characterized by a rejection of what God was trying to do in, for, and through them; the ultimate rejection came in the crucifixion of Jesus and continued in the persecution and martyrdom of His followers.
Outline:
Verses 1-50 – Stephen traced the history of the Jewish nation through the call of Abraham, the Egyptian captivity, the exodus, and the establishment of the nation of Israel to prove that the heritage of the people was one of rebellion and rejection.
Verses 51-53 – Stephen personalized the rebellion to his present audience.
Verses 54-60 – Incensed with anger and guilt, the mob attacked and killed Stephen, who breathed his last breath as a prayer for his executioners.
Prayer Focus: Lord, give me both the intelligence and the spirit of Stephen to confront opposition with wisdom and victorious humility. Amen.
Notes:

Spiritual Journal:

Week: Twenty
Day: Tuesday
Book: Acts
Chapter: Eight
Memory Verse: Eight
Principle: Whether preached in a city-wide crusade to a multitude or shared personally with a lone individual, the message of the gospel is the power of God unto salvation.
Outline:

Verses 1-3 – The disciples buried Stephen as a great persecution began to arise.

Verses 4-8 – Philip traveled to Samaria where he brought a great revival of healing, deliverance, and salvation.

Verses 9-13 – Simon the Magician was converted under Philip's ministry.

Verses 14-25 – When Peter and John came to Samaria to add the ministry of the Holy Spirit to the foundational truths laid by Philip, Simon's true character was revealed as he offered to buy the magical secret of the apostles' ministry. Peter's words of warning brought him to repentance and restoration.

Verses 26-38 – Philip was directed by the Holy Spirit to go into the desert, where he met an Ethiopian traveler who was eager to receive the gospel and be baptized.

Verses 39-40 – Philip was supernaturally translated to Azotus.

Prayer Focus: Lord, make me aware of all the opportunities – great and small – You set before me to share Your gospel. Amen.

Notes:

Spiritual Journal:

Week: Twenty
Day: Wednesday
Book: Acts
Chapter: Nine
Memory Verse: Sixteen
Principle: It has been said that a good motto for life is to expect the unexpected. When living the Spirit-led life, this is especially true, for the God of the impossible is always at work making the unusual, the unexpected, and the impossible part of our daily course of events.
Outline:
        Verses 1-19 – The greatest opponent of the church became one of its greatest proponents.
        Verses 20-30 – The persecutor of Christ began to be persecuted for Him.
        Verse 31 – The church prospered and increased as persecution tried to silence it.
        Verses 32-35 – A man who had been confined to bed for eight years was instantly healed and restored to full health.
        Verses 36-43 – A dead woman was restored to life.
Prayer Focus: Lord, teach me to walk in the unexpected and the miraculous supernatural. Amen.
Notes:

Spiritual Journal:

Week: Twenty
Day: Thursday
Book: Acts
Chapter: Ten
Memory Verse: Thirty-eight
Principle: In the story of the giving of the Holy Spirit to the first gentile converts, Luke confirmed a theme that, even though it ran throughout the whole Old Testament, was not recognized by the Jews: the blessings of God are for all men – not just one individual race.
Outline:
Verses 1-8 – An angel told Cornelius to send for Peter.
Verses 9-16 – Peter received a vision which taught the lesson that the command to be separate was no longer acceptable to God.
Verses 17-23 – Peter was commissioned to go to Cornelius' home without doubting.
Verses 24-33 – Cornelius explained to Peter how he had received the angelic visitation.
Verses 34-43 – Peter preached the gospel of Jesus to Cornelius and his household.
Verses 44-48 – Cornelius and his family were filled with the Holy Spirit and received water baptism.
Prayer Focus: Lord, it is my tendency to prejudge people and separate myself from some of them; help me to always be open and receptive to sharing Your love with all men. Amen.
Notes:

Spiritual Journal:

Week: Twenty
Day: Friday
Book: Acts
Chapter: Eleven
Memory Verse: Nine
Principle: The episodes recounted in this chapter show a mutual acceptance that began –
   although reluctantly – between the Jewish and the gentile believers.
Outline:
> Verses 1-18 – When Peter was called by the church leadership to explain what
> happened at Cornelius' house, the elders were convinced of the validity of
> the ministry to the gentiles.
>
> Verses 19-26 – When the gospel reached as far as Antioch, the believers began to
> evangelize among the non-Jewish Greeks. Barnabas was commissioned
> by the church leadership to minister to these new gentile believers; he also
> drew Saul of Tarsus into this mission.
>
> Verses 27-30 – The aid sent to the saints in Jerusalem as a result of Agabus'
> prophecy illustrated that the gentiles accepted the Jewish leadership and
> were accepted by them.

Prayer Focus: Lord, I've heard the saying that, when someone draws a circle which leaves
   me out, I should draw a bigger one which takes him in; help me to live by this
   principle. Amen.
Notes:

Spiritual Journal:

Week: Twenty-one

Day: Monday

Book: Acts

Chapter: Twelve

Memory Verse: Twenty-four

Principle: Today's memory verse is one of several summary verses which appear throughout the book of Acts confirming that no matter what happens against the church, God continues to cause it to grow and multiply.

Outline:

Verses 1-4 – Political persecution of the church included the execution of James and the intended execution of Peter.

Verses 5-11 – An angel supernaturally released Peter from prison.

Verses 12-19 – Astonished at Peter's miraculous appearance, those who had been interceding for his release were too surprised to let him into the house. Among the guards at the prison, there was equal astonishment at his disappearance.

Verses 20-23 – King Herod was judged by God for his wickedness and pride.

Verse 24 – Luke gives a progress report on the growth of the church.

Verse 25 – John Mark teamed up with Barnabas and Paul.

Prayer Focus: Lord, it is too easy to look at the setbacks rather than the advances in life. Help me to always be aware of the progress You are accomplishing in and through me. Amen.

Notes:

Spiritual Journal:

Week: Twenty-one
Day: Tuesday
Book: Acts
Chapter: Thirteen
Memory Verse: Fifty-two
Principle: The gospel is triumphant against every sort of resistance from any source.
Outline:

> Verses 1-3 – Barnabas and Saul were set apart by the church leadership as the first official missionaries of the Christian faith.
>
> Verses 4-12 – They traveled through the length of the island of Cyprus ministering. One especially notable confrontation took place with a sorcerer who attempted to keep the Roman official from receiving their message.
>
> Verses 13-41 – When they reached Antioch in Pisidia, they were invited to preach in the synagogue there. Paul's message contained the characteristic elements of the sermons recorded in Acts: the history of the Jewish nation emphasizing their resistance to God's plan and the prophets' predictions of the coming of Jesus; however, it did not contain the proclamation of guilt for Jesus' death as did the sermons preached in Jerusalem.
>
> Verses 42-51 – The gentiles received the message of salvation, but the Jews stirred up such a resistance against it that Paul and Barnabas shook the dust of the city off their feet and left.
>
> Verse 52 – Joy and the presence of the Holy Spirit characterized the lives of the disciples.

Prayer Focus: Lord, let me be filled with joy and the Holy Spirit even when resistance arises. Amen.

Notes:

Spiritual Journal:

Week: Twenty-one

Day: Wednesday

Book: Acts

Chapter: Fourteen

Memory Verse: Twenty-two

Principle: We must always keep our eyes on the heaven we are going to rather than on the hell we are going through.

Outline:

Verses 1-7 – Barnabas and Saul had to flee Iconium because of the violence which arose there.

Verses 8-20 – Due to a miracle healing in the city of Lystra, the people wanted to sacrifice to Barnabas and Paul as if they were gods. When they refused this worship, the crowd turned on them and stoned Paul; but God raised him up.

Verses 21-28 – Barnabas and Paul circled back through the cities they had visited to encourage the brethren that, waiting at the end of the tribulation they were enduring, was the Kingdom of God.

Prayer Focus: Lord, never let me lose focus on my final destination – Jesus Christ, the author and finisher of my faith. Amen.

Notes:

Spiritual Journal:

Week: Twenty-one

Day: Thursday

Book: Acts

Chapter: Fifteen

Memory Verse: Nine

Principle: It is often important to meet together and discuss our differences and questions so that we can live and function in unity. You might say that it is important to "put all the cards on the table" so we can all be "on the same page."

Outline:

Verses 1-29 – Barnabas and Saul met with the leadership in Jerusalem to "clear the air" concerning what was to be taught to the new gentile converts. It was decided that they be fully accepted with only limited restrictions:

a) Abstain from meat sacrificed to idols,

b) Abstain from food containing blood,

c) Abstain from meat from strangled animals, and

d) Abstain from sexual immorality.

Verses 30-35 – Paul and Barnabas, along with two representatives from the Jerusalem eldership, returned to Antioch to report on the results of the council meeting.

Verses 36-41 – As they prepared for a second missionary journey, Paul and Barnabas split up over the issue of having John Mark join them. It is interesting how they could be so readily divided after just fighting so powerfully for unity within the church.

Prayer Focus: Lord, help me to be willing to submit myself to the necessary process for airing out issues with my Christian brethren. Amen.

Notes:

Spiritual Journal:

Week: Twenty-one

Day: Friday

Book: Acts

Chapter: Sixteen

Memory Verse: Thirty-one

Principle: God is in charge – whether leading us as to where to go and where not to go or in sending an earthquake to open a prison; if we allow Him to direct our lives, we will see His hand at work in every area.

Outline:

Verses 1-6 – Timothy received circumcision and joined Paul's evangelistic company.

Verses 7-10 – Paul's missionary plans were dictated supernaturally through the leading of the Spirit and divinely-inspired dreams.

Verses 11-15 – Household salvation came to Lydia's family.

Verses 16-24 – The deliverance of a demon-possessed girl landed Paul and Silas in jail.

Verses 25-34 – The miraculous deliverance from the prison resulted in household salvation for the jailer's family.

Verses 35-40 – Paul demanded the rights he deserved as a Roman citizen.

Prayer Focus: Lord, help me to believe for and receive salvation for every member of my family. Amen.

Notes:

Spiritual Journal:

Week: Twenty-two

Day: Monday

Book: Acts

Chapter: Seventeen

Memory Verse: Eleven

Principle: In this chapter, we meet people with dramatically different spiritual mindsets: the Thessalonians who rioted against the gospel, the Bereans who readily received it, the philosophers who debated it and thought it strange, and the few who believed. These individuals demonstrate that no one is unresponsive to the gospel; everyone just responds differently.

Outline:

Verses 1-9 – When the gospel was preached in Thessalonica, the Jews were so enraged that they caused a great uproar in the city.

Verses 10-14 – The people of Berea readily received the Word of the Lord; however, the opponents from Thessalonica came there and stirred up enough trouble that Paul had to leave.

Verses 15-34 – When Paul preached in Athens, he encountered men of diverse backgrounds (from Stoics, who were extremely austere, to Epicurean, who were extremely self-indulgent), yet they all were exceedingly religious. Paul preached to them concerning the one God they had not yet known; their response, for the most part, was that the resurrection from the dead was too strange an idea for them to accept.

Prayer Focus: Lord, of all men, let me be like the Bereans who were noble in their readiness of mind to receive and search the scriptures. Amen.

Notes:

Spiritual Journal:

Week: Twenty-two
Day: Tuesday
Book: Acts
Chapter: Eighteen
Memory Verse: Six
Principle: "Never say, 'Die!'" might be a good way to sum up the truths of this chapter.
Even though the section begins with Paul's shaking the dust off his shoes in
regard to the Jews, it ends with Apollos' mightily convincing them concerning
Jesus.
Outline:
Verses 1-3 – Paul becomes associated with Aquilla and Priscilla.
Verses 4-11 – After Paul acknowledged the Jews' rejection of the gospel, he
began to minister from a gentile home next-door to the Jewish synagogue.
Verses 12-17 – When the Roman governor refused to hear the accusations which
the Jews brought against the Christians; the incensed gentiles attacked the
Jewish leader, but the governor paid no attention.
Verses 18-28 – After Paul planted Aquilla and Priscilla in Ephesus on his way to
Jerusalem, Apollos – a promising new preacher – arrived and learned the
full revelation of the gospel of Jesus from them.
Prayer Focus: Lord, help me when I don't know the full truth about a matter to find a
person like Aquilla or Priscilla who can instruct me more fully.   Amen.
Notes:

Spiritual Journal:

Week: Twenty-two
Day: Wednesday
Book: Acts
Chapter: Nineteen
Memory Verse: Fifteen
Principle: The strength of demonic power is demonstrated in the story of the sons of
Sceva, but the ultimate power of God is demonstrated in the story of the
encounter over the temple of Diana of Ephesus.
Outline:

Verses 1-10 – Paul's ministry of the infilling of the Holy Spirit to twelve of John
the Baptist's disciples resulted in a two-year teaching ministry in the city
of Ephesus.

Verses 11-20 – Paul's ministry was attested to with miraculous signs, while the
self-appointed ministries of Sceva's sons were characterized by utter
defeat.

Verses 21-41 – Demetrius incited a riot against Paul because the preaching of the
gospel had turned too much of his clientele from idol worship; however,
even the Roman government seemed to give a stamp of approval for the
gospel and a disregard for the opposition.

Prayer Focus: Lord, help me to always be aware of the ministry You have given me and
never try to invent my own. Amen.
Notes:

Spiritual Journal:

Week: Twenty-two
Day: Thursday
Book: Acts
Chapter: Twenty
Memory Verse: Twenty-four
Principle: The key to having a successful finale to your life and ministry is to get to the place where the cost of success is not a factor to be considered.
Outline:

Verses 1-5 – Paul made plans and began his final journey to Israel.

Verses 6-12 – Eutychus was raised after his tragic fall during Paul's all-night ministry in Troas.

Verses 13-38 – As Paul continued his journey to Jerusalem, he stopped to emphasize several truths to the believers in the cities along the way:

a) His character demonstrated his call,

b) His commitment demonstrated his commission,

c) His caution demonstrated his concern, and

d) His communion demonstrated his compassion.

Prayer Focus: Lord, help me to be so focused on what lies at the end of my journey that I am not moved by what lies in my path ahead. Amen.
Notes:

Spiritual Journal:

Week: Twenty-two
Day: Friday
Book: Acts
Chapter: Twenty-one
Memory Verse: Thirteen
Principle: Paul's attitude toward his impending arrest and martyrdom displays the principle of victory which will later be penned in Revelation 12:11, "They overcame him (Satan) by the blood of the Lamb and by the word of their testimony; and they loved not their lives unto the death."
Outline:
> Verses 1-14 – As Paul traveled toward Jerusalem, he was continually confronted by prophetic warnings concerning the destiny which awaited him in the Holy City; however, he accepted his fate boldly and was concerned only by the lack of courage displayed by his friends and companions.
>
> Verses 15-26 – Paul was willing to pay any price in order to keep peace and unity within the Body of Christ – even participating in the Jewish Temple sacrifice even though he knew and taught that such rituals were no longer necessary or beneficial for personal salvation.
>
> Verses 27-40 – False accusations shouted by an angry mob in the Temple incited a riot which would have resulted in Paul's being torn limb from limb unless the Romans had taken him into protective custody.

Prayer Focus: Lord, the blood of the Lamb is easy, the word of my testimony is sometimes a little harder, but I really need Your help with being able to not love my own life to the death. Amen.
Notes:

Spiritual Journal:

Week: Twenty-three

Day: Monday

Book: Acts

Chapter: Twenty-two

Memory Verse: Sixteen

Principle: This chapter illustrates a point within another point: the fact that Paul chose to share his testimony when in a life-and-death situation demonstrates the truth that a man with an experience is never at the mercy of a man with an argument. In sharing his testimony, Paul displayed the urgency of following God's directives exactly and without hesitation.

Outline:

Verses 1-23 – Paul shared his testimony with the rioting mob.

Verses 24-30 – The Roman officers became concerned for their own safety when they realized that they had mistreated a fellow Roman citizen.

Prayer Focus: Lord, help me to realize and utilize the power of my personal testimony. Amen.

Notes:

Spiritual Journal:

Week: Twenty-three

Day: Tuesday

Book: Acts

Chapter: Twenty-three

Memory Verse: One

Principle: The unusual way in which the intrigue and covert plot of this chapter are uncovered and settled proves the sovereignty of the God who is in control even when the circumstances don't look like it.

Outline:

Verses 1-5 – When Paul retaliated against the high priest's command that he be struck, the apostle responded that he didn't recognize the office – not that he didn't know that the man was in the position, but that he didn't acknowledge that the man in the office was actually in the position of a priest between God and man.

Verses 6-10 – Paul used the great military tactic of "divide and conquer" when he brought up the question of the resurrection – which was a point of contention between the Sadducees and the Pharisees who made up the council before whom he stood. They became so embroiled in an internal argument that they lost their focus against the apostle.

Verses 11-35 – When the Jews realized that they had allowed Paul to escape their grasp, they plotted to ambush him and execute him outside the legal system. However, an angel had already promised Paul safety, and it was provided when the apostle's nephew heard of the plot and informed the officer who then provided safe passage out of Jerusalem for Paul.

Prayer Focus: Lord, even though I have never had an angel in my bedroom to promise Your protection, I have a Bible on my night stand which proclaims the same promise continually; help me to believe in and experience the provision of living under the shelter of Your wings. Amen.

Notes:

Spiritual Journal:

Week: Twenty-three
Day: Wednesday
Book: Acts
Chapter: Twenty-four
Memory Verse: Fourteen
Principle: Paul's trials verify the promise of Isaiah 54:17 that every tongue which rises against us in judgment shall be condemned.
Outline:
Verses 1-23 – Even though Paul chose to testify on his own behalf when an eminent orator was called in to present the case against him, Felix was unable to find sufficient cause to prosecute Paul.
Verses 24-27 – Hoping for a bribe from the apostle's friends, the governor allowed Paul to remain incarcerated for two years.
Prayer Focus: Lord, help me to live my life as I Peter 2:20 teaches so that any prosecution I may encounter will be because of my good deeds, not evil doings.   Amen.
Notes:

Spiritual Journal:

Week: Twenty-three

Day: Thursday

Book: Acts

Chapter: Twenty-five

Memory Verse: Eleven

Principle: Paul's trial before Festus confirms the principle established in Daniel 12:3 and Matthew 23:42 that believers shall shine forth in their righteousness.

Outline:

Verses 1-5 – When a new Roman official was placed in power, the Jewish leaders took the occasion as a new opportunity to ambush Paul; yet, the governor insisted that the accusers come to the Roman headquarters in Caesarea for a legal hearing.

Verses 6-12 – When Festus realized that the civil trial in Caesarea was pointless, he suggested that Paul be re-tried in a religious hearing in Jerusalem; at this point, Paul exercised his right of citizenship to appeal his trial to Rome.

Verses 13-27 – Lacking just cause to send Paul to the appellate court in Rome, Festus arranged a hearing before the Jewish king to help clarify charges to list against the prisoner.

Prayer Focus: Lord, I want to be like Paul, who in his own life demonstrated the principle which he taught in I Timothy 3:7 when he instructed those who would represent Christ to be of a good report among those who are outside the community of faith. Amen.

Notes:

Spiritual Journal:

Week: Twenty-three

Day: Friday

Book: Acts

Chapter: Twenty-six

Memory Verse: Nineteen

Principle: As Paul recounts his testimony before Agrippa, he stresses the fact that a person who has an encounter with Jesus that results in a changed life should not become static or stagnant; rather, he should be vibrantly aggressive in the Kingdom of God.

Outline:

Verses 1-12 – Paul told of his misdirected zeal as a Jewish leader.

Verses 13-18 – Paul testified of his eye-opening encounter with Jesus who changed the direction of his life.

Verses 19-23 – Paul briefly recapped the new mission he launched into after his conversion.

Verses 24-26 – Festus responded to Paul's testimony by saying that he must be insane.

Verses 27-32 – Agrippa responded to Paul's testimony by saying that the man was not guilty and could have been released except that his destiny was already set to go to Rome.

Prayer Focus: Lord, help me to always be clear as to what the heavenly vision for my life is and to never become disobedient to it. Amen.

Notes:

Spiritual Journal:

Week: Twenty-four

Day: Monday

Book: Acts

Chapter: Twenty-seven

Memory Verse: Twenty-five

Principle: Even when the Lord's followers are tossed in the storms of life and when they encounter shipwreck, the angel of the Lord is with them just as the fourth man was seen in the fiery furnace with the three Hebrew witnesses in Babylon.

Outline:

Verses 1-13 – Since Paul (according to II Corinthians 11:25) had already endured three shipwrecks, he should have been recognized as somewhat of an authority on the matter of storms at sea; however, his advice against sailing at this time was unheeded by the captain, the centurion, and the ship's owner.

Verses 14-44 – After the storm engulfed the ship, Paul's words became important to the passengers and crew of the ill-fated vessel.

a) He inspired them with the word from the angelic messenger.

b) His command kept everyone inside the boat.

c) His example encouraged them to eat and regain their strength.

d) His presence saved the prisoners from execution.

Prayer Focus: Lord, I'd love to be able to be heard without going through a storm at sea and a shipwreck; but, if that's what it takes, help me to be willing.   Amen.

Notes:

Spiritual Journal:

Week: Twenty-four
Day: Tuesday
Book: Acts
Chapter: Twenty-eight
Memory Verse: Thirty-one
Principle: Even though the book of Acts seems to come to an abrupt end with no formal conclusion, it seems that the closing remarks emphasize the spirit of not only the book but the heart of God and the experience of the church: even in every kind of opposition, the gospel is unhindered!
Outline:
> Verses 1-10 – The miraculous deliverance from the venom of the viper and the healing of the governor's father gave the shipwrecked Paul a place of respect on the island of Malta.
>
> Verses 11-16 – Even though he was a prisoner, Paul was granted the respect of being able to visit with friends along the way and was honored by an escort of believers as he entered Rome.
>
> Verses 17-24 – Paul arranged a hearing with the Jewish leaders in Rome, who received him without hostility and listened intently to his testimony and teachings.
>
> Verses 25-29 – Paul concluded that it was prophetic that the gospel should be preached to the gentiles.
>
> Verses 30-31 – Paul's two years under house arrest in Rome were characterized by his continued ministry.

Prayer Focus: Lord, help me to be a continual example of the church triumphant. Amen.
Notes:

Spiritual Journal:

Week: Twenty-four
Day: Wednesday
Book: Romans
Chapter: One
Memory Verse: Sixteen
Principle: Paul's letter to the Romans contains a rather lengthy systematic theology which begins with an explanation that all men have a revelation of the gospel and are without excuse for rejecting it.
Outline:
Verses 1-7 – In this introductory statement, Paul introduced himself as a servant, an apostle, and a called-out one; he gave a definition of the uniqueness of the gospel; and he greeted the Romans by extending grace and peace to them.

Verses 8-15 – Paul emphasized his desire and determination to come to Rome to minister to the believers there.

Verses 16-18 – Paul projected the power of the gospel to bring salvation against the background that there is a natural revelation of God's righteousness to those of faith and of His wrath toward the unrighteous.

Verses 19-23 – Paul explained that there is a natural revelation of God's nature and His requirements, yet men have rejected this knowledge and rebelled against it.

Verses 24-32 – Paul described the deplorable state of man as a result of his rejection of the natural revelation of God.

Prayer Focus: Lord, help me to never reject the revelation You have left for me.   Amen.
Notes:

Spiritual Journal:

Week: Twenty-four
Day: Thursday
Book: Romans
Chapter: Two
Memory Verse: Twenty-nine
Principle: In this chapter, Paul turned to the Jews and showed that they, too, were without
   excuse because they refused the special revelation given to them – just as the
   gentiles had rejected the natural revelation which they had been given.
Outline:
   Verses 1-11 – Paul explained that, because of God's impartiality, He will judge
     the Jews just as readily – even more so – as the gentiles.
   Verses 12-16 – Every man has the law of God and the awareness of right and
     wrong in his heart – whether from having learned it or from having it
     naturally revealed in the universe around him.
   Verses 17-29 – Paul exposed the hypocrisy and self-righteousness of the Jews and
     called them to a realization of the heart requirements which God had
     placed on them.
Prayer Focus: Lord, help me to always remember that I have no excuse if I ever try to
   rely on anything other than the inward righteousness which You work in my life.
   Amen.
Notes:

Spiritual Journal:

Week: Twenty-four
Day: Friday
Book: Romans
Chapter: Three
Memory Verse: Twenty-five
Principle: Once he was able to conclude that all men are sinners, Paul was able to present God's glorious solution to the sin problem – the propitiation of Christ!
Outline:

> Verses 1-2 – Paul explained that there was a genuine advantage to the Jews' having special revelation versus the gentiles' position with only natural revelation.

> Verses 3-20 – Paul next answered the questions concerning the failure of the special revelation to bring about a righteous people, by showing that man's failure did not disqualify the special revelation of law but rather established it by painting it on the canvas of man's utterly sinful nature.

> Verses 21-26 – Jesus' propitiation, or eradication of sin and guilt, can only be revealed against the background of the fact that all men are included in the summation of sin.

> Verses 27-31 – Salvation as a work of God eliminates man's right to boast in any goodness of his own.

Prayer Focus: Lord, help me to always remember that I am one of those who is also included under Your summation that all men are sinners and that it is only through Your grace, not my goodness, that I am saved. Amen.

Notes:

Spiritual Journal:

Week: Twenty-five
Day: Monday
Book: Romans
Chapter: Four
Memory Verse: Fourteen
Principle: Having used the previous three chapters to establish the principle that all men are sinners, Paul now turns to the promise of salvation, with this chapter focusing on the truth that it cannot be earned through righteous works.
Outline:
>Verses 1-3 – Abraham received justification through faith.
>
>Verses 4-5 – For all men, faith is the key to righteousness.
>
>Verses 6-8 – David confirmed that God imputes righteousness independent of man's works.
>
>Verses 9-12 – God's promises are not dependent upon circumcision, which symbolizes adherence to Jewish law.
>
>Verses 13-21 – By faith, Abraham obtained the promises of God.
>
>Verses 22-25 – The principles demonstrated in Abraham's life were not unique to him; they were examples for our lives as well.

Prayer Focus: Lord, help me to receive that imputed righteousness and not try to earn my salvation, but I also ask that You help me not to abuse the grace of God by continuing to live deliberately in sin.   Amen.
Notes:

Spiritual Journal:

Week: Twenty-five
Day: Tuesday
Book: Romans
Chapter: Five
Memory Verse: One
Principle: In this chapter, Paul establishes the point that, just as man's sinful state is totally the result of Adam's sin, salvation is totally dependent upon the obedience of Jesus Christ.
Outline:

Verses 1-5 – Paul listed a chain-reaction of benefits of salvation:

a) Justification,
b) Peace with God,
c) Faith,
d) Grace,
e) Ability to stand,
f) Ability to rejoice,
g) Hope,
h) Ability to glory in tribulation,
i) Patience,
j) Experience,
k) another level of hope,
l) Being unashamed,
m) Love, and
n) The Holy Spirit.

Verses 6-11 – Paul pointed out that, certainly, Christ is willing to give benefits to us as believers since He willingly died for us while we were His enemies.

Verses 12-21 – The destructive work of Adam was remedied by the saving act of Jesus.

Prayer Focus: Lord, help me to be able to receive all the benefits of Your salvation. Amen.

Notes:

Spiritual Journal:

Week: Twenty-five
Day: Wednesday
Book: Romans
Chapter: Six
Memory Verse: Fourteen
Principle: Having established the believer's position in the righteousness of Christ, Paul turned in this chapter to explain the believer's attitude toward sin and to demonstrate the victory we have over it.
Outline:
Verses 1-11 – Paul used the analogy of death to describe the believer's relationship to sin – just as a dead man is not affected by the environment, a Christian is no longer under the influence of sin.
Verses 12-16 – Paul proclaimed that the believer must take an active stance of resistance against sin.
Verses 17-23 – Paul illustrated our former relationship to sin and our present relationship with righteousness in terms of a servant with his master and the wages of his labor.
Prayer Focus: Lord, I admit that it is easy to allow that former master, sin, to continue to exert authority over me; help me to realize that I am no longer his slave. Amen.
Notes:

Spiritual Journal:

Week: Twenty-five
Day: Thursday
Book: Romans
Chapter: Seven
Memory Verse: Twenty-two
Principle: The Old Testament law was meant as a mirror to reveal man's need for righteousness, but it proved to be a magnifying glass focusing on his sinfulness.
Outline:

        Verses 1-6 – Paul again employed the analogy of death to help explain the Christian's position; this time, he turned to the authority of the Law and stated that believers are no more bound to the ordinances of the Law than a widow is bound to her dead husband.

        Verses 7-14 – Paul explained that the Law, in and of itself, is not evil, but the sinfulness of man turned the goodness of the Law into a weapon of destruction targeting the men it should have blessed.

        Verses 15-23 – Paul found himself in the personal dilemma of doing the bad things which he determined not to do and not doing the good things he desired to do.

        Verses 24-25 – He realized that his only hope of deliverance was through Jesus Christ.

Prayer Focus: Lord, thank You that You have provided a way of deliverance for me; help me to always appropriate it.   Amen.

Notes:

Spiritual Journal:

Week: Twenty-five

Day: Friday

Book: Romans

Chapter: Eight

Memory Verse: One

Principle: The Christian's victory lies in having the Holy Spirit actively involved in his life; this truth is dramatically demonstrated in that the Spirit is rarely mentioned prior to this chapter but is referenced repeatedly in this one chapter.

Outline:

Verses 1-5 – Paul explained the contrast of the condemnation of the law of sin and death through the flesh with the liberation of the law of life through the spirit.

Verses 6-13 – The apostle explained that while being fleshly minded will kill a person, the person can kill the deeds of the flesh and have life.

Verses 14-25 – The Spirit proclaims our relationship to God as sons, the redemption for which the entire universe is waiting.

Verses 26-28 – When we allow the Holy Spirit to intercede over our situations, we know that they will work out to our best interest.

Verses 29-33 – God has a good plan for our lives which He had prearranged even before we came into His family.

Verses 34-39 – Because of God's love and plan for us, we can believe that we will be victorious no matter what comes or goes.

Prayer Focus: Lord, I welcome Your Holy Spirit to live in and through me to make me the victorious believer You want me to be. Amen.

Notes:

Spiritual Journal:

Week: Twenty-six

Day: Monday

Book: Romans

Chapter: Nine

Memory Verse: Fifteen

Principle: Through the use of Old Testament examples, Paul illustrates the truth that it is God, not man, who is in charge of the plan of eternal salvation.

Outline:

Verses 1-5 – Paul expressed his willingness to give himself for the salvation of the Jewish people, who were in line for God's blessings.

Verses 6-13 – Paul explained that the blessings of God are not automatic in the physical bloodline, but are based on divine election.

Verses 14-24 – He defended the sovereignty of God's election.

Verses 25-33 – Paul pointed to lack of faith as the factor which kept Israel from receiving the fulfillment of God's promises.

Prayer Focus: Lord, I understand that it is lack of faith and obedience on the part of the many called ones that keeps them from being included among the few chosen ones; help me to be both called and chosen. Amen.

Notes:

Spiritual Journal:

Week: Twenty-six
Day: Tuesday
Book: Romans
Chapter: Ten
Memory Verse: Nine
Principle: The failure of the Jewish nation to obtain salvation illustrates the truth that religion cannot replace faith.
Outline:
> Verses 1-3 – The Jewish nation failed to obtain salvation because they lacked the knowledge that Jesus was God's plan for salvation.
>
> Verse 4 – Christ ended the Law.
>
> Verses 5-13 – God's plan of salvation – for Jew or gentile – has always been based on heart belief and oral confession.
>
> Verses 14-21 – The message was preached to – but rejected by – the Jews, while some of the gentiles – who had not even sought for it – received the gospel.

Prayer Focus: Lord, how tragic it is to think of the ones who have not believed because they have not heard due to lack of a preacher, but how much more tragic to think of those who have heard but failed to believe and receive; help me to accept Your gospel for my own salvation and then enable me to communicate it to those who have not yet heard.   Amen.

Notes:

Spiritual Journal:

Week: Twenty-six
Day: Wednesday
Book: Romans
Chapter: Eleven
Memory Verse: Twenty-nine
Principle: Set against the background of the previous chapters, the promise of hope for Israel's restoration and salvation in this passage is especially refreshing. Alongside this promise, a sobering warning is given to the gentiles that their election, as described for Israel earlier, is tenuous, in that it is based on their continued faith in and obedience to Christ.

Outline:

Verses 1-6 – Paul explained that, even though the nation of Israel had turned away from God, their rebellion was not universal and a redeemed remnant remained.

Verses 7-16 – If the plan of redemption for the gentiles was a part of the purpose of the rejection of Israel, how much more will the redemption of Israel result in the salvation of the nations.

Verses 17-24 – Paul illustrated the principle with an analogy of branches being grafted into and pruned from an olive tree, showing that God can include or exclude at His own will.

Verses 25-36 – Paul summed up the discussion of God's sovereignty with an explanation of His unsearchable mercy, which includes the eventual plan that all Israel will be saved and restored.

Prayer Focus: Lord, I cast myself on Your unfathomable mercy to receive Your immeasurable grace and eternal salvation.   Amen.

Notes:

Spiritual Journal:

Week: Twenty-six
Day: Thursday
Book: Romans
Chapter: Twelve
Memory Verse: Two
Principle: Because of God's unfathomable mercy, which has included us in His best plans even though we deserve the worst, we must renew our minds so our lives will demonstrate His perfect plan.
Outline:

      Verses 1-2 – Paul besought the believers to be transformed from worldly thinking and be renewed to heavenly thinking.

      Verses 3-8 – Each person has a specific place to serve in the Body of Christ and a specific ministry to fulfill.

      Verses 9-21 – Certain attitudes and actions are characteristic of the person who has been transformed into the Kingdom of God.

Prayer Focus: Lord, I want to transform my thinking, actions, and lifestyle to conform to Your Kingdom so that I'll not be conformed to the present world system.   Amen.
Notes:

Spiritual Journal:

Week: Twenty-six
Day: Friday
Book: Romans
Chapter: Thirteen
Memory Verse: One
Principle: Having talked about how believers are supposed to live within the Body of Christ, Paul broadened the scope by including the role of the Christian in society as a whole; it is important for a Christian to see that he is part of society, not a separate and opposing force outside human institutions, even though he may be in opposition to the system of the world.

Outline:

Verses 1-7 – Paul reminded the Christians of their responsibility to obey the government based on the facts that the government was in place because of God's plan and purpose, that they could justly be punished because of disobedience, and that they were to keep a clean conscience before God at all times and in relationship to all things – including their obedience to the ruling powers.

Verses 8-10 – Paul demonstrated how the laws of God actually dictated the laws of society.

Verses 11-14 – Paul concluded this discussion with a challenge and admonition to live not only by Christian principles, but by and through Christ Himself.

Prayer Focus: Lord, it is hard to see all authority as being in place by Your design, but I submit myself to viewing it as so; help me to live by Your laws and, therefore, fulfill the laws of man. Amen.

Notes:

Spiritual Journal:

Week: Twenty-seven
Day: Monday
Book: Romans
Chapter: Fourteen
Memory Verse: Seventeen
Principle: Paul reiterated that the true character of the law-abiding personality is a pure heart, not actual rules and regulations that are followed externally.
Outline:
> Verse 1 – Paul admonished that the weaker believers should be accepted, but not through compromise.
>
> Verses 2-9 – Paul explained that some regulations are negotiable as long as they do not violate the specific commandments and general nature of God.
>
> Verses 10-13 – Every man is responsible individually to God for his own actions and attitudes.
>
> Verses 14-21 – Paul explained that specific acts were not as significant as a heart which is pure toward God and a spirit which is sensitive toward others.
>
> Verses 22-23 – Anything done through a doubtful heart is to be considered as sin.

Prayer Focus: Lord, open my spiritual eyes so I can see the true nature of righteousness and sinfulness as easily as I can read the printed law with my physical eyes. Amen.

Notes:

Spiritual Journal:

Week: Twenty-seven
Day: Tuesday
Book: Romans
Chapter: Fifteen
Memory Verse: Thirteen
Principle: Acceptance of members from different races and backgrounds is necessary within the Body of Christ for acceptance of the Body by Christ.
Outline:

Verses 1-7 – It is the responsibility of those who consider themselves to be strong in the Lord to demonstrate acceptance of others and develop unity of thought and word within the church.

Verses 8-12 – Paul used Old Testament scriptures to verify God's prophetic intention to include the gentiles in the Body of Christ.

Verses 13-16 – The apostle admonished the believers that they should not only receive the blessings of God but also become ministers of these blessings to the gentiles.

Verses 17-28 – He explained his own ministry in terms of his effective outreach to the gentiles and his continued determination to expand the scope of his influence; he added that the gentiles had collected a bountiful offering to support the Jerusalem church, proving their commitment to the church.

Verses 29-33 – Paul expressed his desire to come to the church at Rome with a blessing and to have the prayer of blessing extended toward him by the church.

Prayer Focus: Lord, help me to never see anything except Jesus in my brothers and sisters in Christ; that way, I'll be able to always readily accept each of them.   Amen.
Notes:

Spiritual Journal:

Week: Twenty-seven
Day: Wednesday
Book: Romans
Chapter: Sixteen
Memory Verse: Twenty
Principle: Each individual within the Body of Christ is important, possessing unique qualities and filling a specific niche.
Outline:

Verses 1-16 – As Paul listed a number of individuals within the Roman church whom he knew, he mentioned their individual uniqueness.

Verses 17-18 – Unfortunately, Paul was also forced to mention that some are destroyers, rather than builders, of the Body of Christ.

Verses 19-20 – He added a simple, but powerful, promise that good will prevail over evil.

Verses 21-23 – Paul concluded the discussion by mentioning more of the positive members of the Body of Christ.

Verses 24-27 – He closed the letter with a pronouncement of blessing.

Prayer Focus: Lord, help me to see the unique value of each and every individual. Amen.

Notes:

Spiritual Journal:

Week: Twenty-seven

Day: Thursday

Book: I Corinthians

Chapter: One

Memory Verse: Eighteen

Principle: It is often easy to get our focus on the wrong thing – such as issues, arguments, and personalities – and fail to retain the gospel of Jesus as the focal point.

Outline:

Verses 1-3 – Paul opened the letter with a formal introduction of himself, a warm greeting to the church, and a theological statement.

Verses 4-9 – He followed up with a thanksgiving for the blessing that is already resident in the church.

Verses 10-17 – Next, he addressed the issue of division among the believers who had segregated themselves according to their favorite teachers and teachings.

Verses 18-25 – Paul explained that the gospel of the crucifixion may seem weak and foolish, but it is the power and wisdom of God.

Verses 26-31 – He reminded the Corinthians that they – in their own nature – were just ordinary men, but Christ had brought them to a super-ordinary existence in which they should glory in Him.

Prayer Focus: Lord, it is easy to get off center and let issues rather than Christ be my focus or to begin to glory in myself rather than in You; help me to find the focal point and not waiver from it. Amen.

Notes:

Spiritual Journal:

Week: Twenty-seven

Day: Friday

Book: I Corinthians

Chapter: Two

Memory Verse: Two

Principle: The only true wisdom is the gospel of the crucifixion – which Paul has described as "foolishness" to the human mind.

Outline:

  Verses 1-8 – Paul reminded the church that his personal ministry had not been with well-prepared speeches and great oratory, but with the simple gospel, which is the wisdom and power of God.

  Verses 9-16 – He instructed the church that it is only through the work of the Holy Spirit that the hidden mysteries of the simple gospel message can be revealed to the believer.

Prayer Focus: Lord, please release the Holy Spirit into my life to reveal to me the hidden mysteries and power of the simple gospel of the crucifixion. Amen.

Notes:

Spiritual Journal:

Week: Twenty-eight

Day: Monday

Book: I Corinthians

Chapter: Three

Memory Verse: Twenty-three

Principle: By remembering that I belong to Christ and that all who are in Christ belong to God, it is easy to bring all other relationships into proper balance.

Outline:

Verses 1-3 – Paul rebuked the church for their lack of spiritual maturity, saying that they were childish and carnal.

Verses 4-8 – He addressed the hero worship and the divisions it had caused within the church, saying that it was the symptom which revealed their lack of spiritual maturity and lack of understanding that everything and everyone must be seen as belonging to Christ and God.

Verses 9-15 – He turned to the analogy of a building to explain that all human effort outside the leading and enabling of God is futile and will be judged by God.

Verses 16-17 – Next, he explained that the true building he is referring to is the temple of God which we are to become.

Verses 18-23 – Man's own wisdom is foolishness and destructive, but recognizing our position in Christ makes everything ours.

Prayer Focus: Lord, I must confess that I really enjoy relying on my own wisdom, but I also realize that it is limited and fruitless; help me to abandon myself to Your wisdom alone. Amen.

Notes:

Spiritual Journal:

Week: Twenty-eight

Day: Tuesday

Book: I Corinthians

Chapter: Four

Memory Verse: Seven

Principle: Like balloons, Christians may sometimes discover that they are simply "full of hot air" and that they are really nothing when deflated; it takes an honest evaluation of oneself and his relationship with Christ to avoid becoming puffed up.

Outline:

Verses 1-5 – Paul reminded the church that God's evaluation, not man's judgment, is what counts.

Verses 6-14 – Paul used himself and Apollos in an exaggerated contrast with the opinions the church members had of themselves to show them how erroneous they were with their puffed-up attitudes.

Verses 15-21 – He corrected them and warned them that he would further reprimand them if they continued in their puffed up attitudes and opinions.

Prayer Focus: Lord, help me to always see myself as You see me – victorious, yet not inflated. Amen.

Notes:

Spiritual Journal:

Week: Twenty-eight
Day: Wednesday
Book: I Corinthians
Chapter: Five
Memory Verse: Six
Principle: Sinners within the church must not go unchecked; sinners outside the church must not go unwarned.
Outline:
Verses 1-2 – Two problems within the church were confronted: a man who was living in incest with his stepmother and the church's boastful attitude toward the situation.
Verses 3-5 – Paul challenged the church to confront the man for his blatant sin.
Verses 6-8 – Paul confronted the church for their blatant arrogance.
Verses 9-11 – Paul corrected the church for thinking that they were to refrain from interacting with sinners in the outside world; he commanded them, rather, to be careful not to condone sin within the church by extending ready fellowship to sinning members.
Verses 12-13 – The church is put on notice to judge error within itself.
Prayer Focus: Lord, help me to be bold and discerning enough to judge rather than condone sin within the church – especially within myself.   Amen.
Notes:

Spiritual Journal:

Week: Twenty-eight
Day: Thursday
Book: I Corinthians
Chapter: Six
Memory Verse: Twenty
Principle: The church, if functioning according to biblical standards, has within itself a system of checks and balances to judge and purify itself; likewise, the individual believer is expected to maintain a self-monitoring attitude.
Outline:

Verses 1-8 – Paul scolded the church for allowing members to take differences to the secular courts, explaining that the church should be the clearinghouse for all differences between members.

Verses 9-11 – He reminded them of where they had come from: unredeemed individuals outside God's inheritance.

Verses 12-18 – Paul used the natural necessity of food and the natural desire for sexual fulfillment to illustrate the principle that, although we are in bodies created for earthly life, we are not created for abusive use of those natural desires and functions; such abuses will be judged and must be shunned.

Verses 19-20 – He capped off his argument with the ultimatum that we no longer have authority over our own bodies because Christ has purchased all rights in the lives of believers.

Prayer Focus: Lord, I do so much desire to honor You in my body and spirit; help me to do all that I do to the glory of God.   Amen.
Notes:

Spiritual Journal:

Week: Twenty-eight

Day: Friday

Book: I Corinthians

Chapter: Seven

Memory Verse: Seventeen

Principle: Second only to salvation, marriage is the most important decision a person will ever make; it must be made with God's guidance and maintained with His blessing.

Outline:

Verses 1-2 – Paul began to answer a question concerning marriage by making the point that it is best to remain single.

Verses 3-6 – He added his personal advice that the married couple is not to hold back on fulfilling each other's physical needs except by mutual agreement for purposes of prayer and fasting.

Verses 7-9 – He reiterated his opinion that the single state is preferable.

Verses 10-16 – Next, the apostle shares a mandate from God (not just his personal advice) that Christians should not divorce unless the unbeliever desires to be released from the partnership, citing the possibility that the believing partner might win the unbeliever.

Verses 17-24 – Paul noted that each person has his own calling as to whether to live single or married, but advised that each one maintain the status in which he was called.

Verses 25-35 – Based on the conditions of the present time, Paul called for believers to put marriage in second place to evangelism, giving full attention to the things of the Lord rather than to family matters.

Verses 36-40 – Paul concluded the discussion with a reminder that marriage is not wrong but that it is his personal opinion, which he thinks is also agreeable with the Spirit of God, that singleness may be a happier state.

Prayer Focus: Lord, help me to know what Your specific calling is for my personal life and fulfill it totally, regardless of what state that might be.   Amen.

Notes:

Spiritual Journal:

Week: Twenty-nine
Day: Monday
Book: I Corinthians
Chapter: Eight
Memory Verse: Nine
Principle: Causing offense for a brother is ultimately more important than whether a thing is literally right or wrong for me as an individual.
Outline:

> Verses 1-3 – When Paul turned to the next question, he began the discussion by getting directly to the heart of the matter – the difference between having an inflated ego over knowing what is right and wrong and having a simple heart of love that prefers a brother's feelings over one's own rights.

> Verses 4-8 – Even though there is no power in an idol to actually defile the meat presented before it, there is power in an individual's conscience to defile him when the meat is set before him if he is unsure in his heart about receiving it.

> Verses 9-13 – Paul concluded that the real sin associated with eating meat which had been presented to idols wasn't in the eating of the meat itself but in damaging the conscience of weaker believers by eating it with disregard for their consciences.

Prayer Focus: Lord, help me to no longer live for myself – and not just for You – but also for others.   Amen.
Notes:

Spiritual Journal:

Week: Twenty-nine
Day: Tuesday
Book: I Corinthians
Chapter: Nine
Memory Verse: Nineteen
Principle: Who you are, what you have, or what you do is only important in view of how positively it affects others.
Outline:

Verses 1-6 – Paul defended his claim to apostleship.

Verses 7-11 – He defended his right to receive financial support from the church.

Verses 12-18 – He then explained that he had imposed neither his apostleship nor his right to support upon the believers because he wanted to minister to them without giving them any platform of accusation against him.

Verses 19-23 – He explained that, in each individual situation, he lived the life that would cause the people to whom he ministered to most readily respond.

Verses 24-27 – He closed this discussion with the analogy of a race, saying that he was running not only with the finish line in sight but also with the rules in mind so that he wouldn't disqualify himself; even though he lived so as to fit each situation in which he ministered, he was careful not to compromise what is right and wrong.

Prayer Focus: Lord, I do want to win those around me to You; give me the wisdom to know how to best relate to each one and the boldness to do so without betraying the faith for which I stand. Amen.

Notes:

Spiritual Journal:

Week: Twenty-nine
Day: Wednesday
Book: I Corinthians
Chapter: Ten
Memory Verse: Twenty-three

Principle: Religious rituals, in and of themselves, can be powerless; however, the spiritual connection obtained through the ritual may be of ultimate strength. The Hebrews of the Old Testament figuratively partook of baptism and communion, yet their lives were not changed because they did not enter into true spiritual fellowship with God. However, eating meat sacrificed to idols can become a source of spiritual bondage if the individual accepts the fellowship of the demonic forces behind the idol.

Outline:

Verses 1-6 – The Old Testament Jews were examples of the fact that a person can go through a religious ceremony and still be a siner by nature.

Verses 7-14 – Paul challenged the Christians to learn from the examples of the past and to be careful to live righteous lives, especially in relationship to idolatry. He encouraged the believers that God was with them to help them through times of temptation.

Verses 15-22 – He explained that the problem faced by the believer was a question of spiritual fellowship – indicating that, just as Christian communion is fellowship with God, partaking in pagan meals could be fellowship with demonic forces.

Verses 23-26 – Paul clarified the question about eating meat which had been purchased from stores where food which had been sacrificed to idols was sold; he explained that the bounty of the earth – including that meat – was from God and intended for the blessing of His people.

Verses 27-33 – He reminded his readers of one important condition concerning their freedom to eat the questioned meat: be certain not to offend anyone watching you.

Prayer Focus: Lord, help me not to trust in my rituals and not to abuse my freedoms; I want to live in vital fellowship with You. Amen.

Notes:

Spiritual Journal:

Week: Twenty-nine

Day: Thursday

Book: I Corinthians

Chapter: Eleven

Memory Verse: Twenty-six

Principle: There must be proper order within the church to ensure spiritual accuracy and social stability.

Outline:

Verses 1-2 – Paul commended the church for following the instruction he had given them as a result of his obedience to Christ.

Verses 3-16 – Paul addressed the role of women within the church by stating that they must be in proper submission to their husbands, just as the husbands must be in proper submission to Christ, who is in proper submission to the Father. He explained that a woman's hair can serve as a symbol of her submission to her husband, but he added that there is no hard-and-fast rule in place in the church concerning this custom.

Verses 17-19 – Next, Paul turned to the issue of improper conduct concerning communion, but stated that the errors only helped to point out and accentuate what is approvable.

Verses 20-26 – Paul reprimanded the believers for allowing the communion service to become a social event rather than a time to remember the sacrificial death of the Lord.

Verses 27-34 – Paul admonished the believers that the communion time must be a time of self-reflection, dedication, and correction; else, it will serve as a point of judgment in their lives.

Prayer Focus: Lord, help me at times of communion – and always – to live a properly self-examined life so that You will find no fault when You examine it. Amen.

Notes:

Spiritual Journal:

Week: Twenty-nine
Day: Friday
Book: I Corinthians
Chapter: Twelve
Memory Verse: Seven
Principle: The proper understanding of spiritual gifts and ministries is that they work to unify and edify the Body of Christ as a whole rather than to draw attention to select individuals.
Outline:
>Verses 1-3 – Paul began his discussion of spiritual manifestations by insisting that they were not to be seen as the same experiences which former pagans would remember from their spiritualist encounters.

>Verses 4-7 – He explained that there are three areas of spiritual manifestation: gifts (supernatural abilities), administrations (divinely appointed people through whom these gifts function), and operations (godly attitudes which motivate those who function in the gifts); these three areas are under the direct authority of the individual members of the Trinity. Even though they are distributed among the individuals of the Body of Christ, when properly manifested, they serve to bless the Body as a whole.

>Verses 8-11 – When Paul listed the spiritual gifts, he added that different individuals may have more than one of these supernatural gifts as the Holy Spirit would desire.

>Verses 12-27 – He illustrated the Body of Christ by comparing it to a human body and explaining how each part is necessary for the whole to function properly.

>Verses 28-30 – The administrations – individuals who are appointed to specific roles within the church – are listed and it is stressed that not everyone can fulfill any specific role.

>Verse 31 – Paul encouraged the believers to seek to function in the gifts but also to truly focus on the quality which he will discuss in the next chapter.

Prayer Focus: Lord, help me to know my gift (or gifts) and position of administration in the Body of Christ and to be able to rely upon Your divine ability to serve properly. Amen.
Notes:

Spiritual Journal:

Week: Thirty
Day: Monday
Book: I Corinthians
Chapter: Thirteen
Memory Verse: Thirteen
Principle: No matter how great the ability or how important the position, nothing of value to the Kingdom of God will be produced without the godly quality of love as the motivation.
Outline:
Verses 1-3 – Paul listed several of the gifts and administrations and concluded that they were without profit and would accomplish nothing without the motivational force of love.

Verses 4-8 – The excellent qualities of love are listed.

Verses 9-12 – Paul explained that we still live in an incomplete world awaiting perfection to come. Although He doesn't specifically state that the "perfect one" he mentions is Christ at His Second Coming, it is generally assumed that this was his intention. Only at that point will perfect love be possible among imperfect humans.

Verse 13 – Faith, hope, and love (with love as the greatest) are the forces which will sustain the church until the arrival of that which is perfect.

Prayer Focus: Lord, help me to live by that more excellent way of love until all things are brought to fruition with the coming of the perfect one. Amen.

Notes:

Spiritual Journal:

Week: Thirty
Day: Tuesday
Book: I Corinthians
Chapter: Fourteen
Memory Verse: Three
Principle: As a general "rule of thumb" the manifestation of any spiritual function can be evaluated by one simple question: "Does it encourage, build up, or comfort the Body of Christ?"

Outline:

Verse 1 – Paul emphasized that, while seeking to manifest the spiritual gifts through love, prophecy should be seen as the foremost gift.

Verses 2-25 – Paul explained that there can be abuses (such as not having an interpretation so that the believers can be edified or such that outsiders are confused) associated with the spiritual gift of speaking in tongues; yet he added that there are many benefits such as a strong personal prayer and worship life, a personal edification, and a message for the church which becomes prophetic when interpreted. He emphasized that the proper place for most tongues speaking was in private devotions rather than in public assemblies.

Verses 26-33 – Paul explained that some simple rules concerning the functioning of spiritual gifts would insure that everything would function to edify the church: limit the number of messages in tongues, make sure that each one is interpreted, make sure that the prophecies are judged and that no one interrupts anyone else, and remember that the prophet is in control of his gift (he does not need to be out-of-control to function in a spiritual manifestation).

Verses 34-35 – The issue of having the women remain silent in the church probably originated from the Jewish custom of having the women seated separately from the men and from the fact that women in that period of time were usually not educated. Therefore, it would have been easy for them to disrupt a church service if they were allowed to ask their husbands for explanations when the minister brought up points they didn't understand.

Verses 36-40 – Paul challenged the Corinthians to follow his rules in their worship with special emphasis on allowing freedom for the spiritual gifts to be manifested while guarding the mandate to keep order.

Prayer Focus: Lord, may all that I do and say bring edification, exhortation, and comfort to the Body of Christ. Amen.

Notes and Spiritual Journal:

Week: Thirty
Day: Wednesday
Book: I Corinthians
Chapter: Fifteen
Memory Verse: Fifty-eight
Principle: We must live our Christian lives in view of the fact that Christ has been resurrected and that we too will be resurrected to eternal life with Him.
Outline:

> Verses 1-11 – Paul reminded the believers of the historical fact of the resurrection based on the number of witnesses of the resurrected Lord.
>
> Verses 12-19 – The resurrection is the pivotal truth of the Christian faith; if there is no resurrection, the entire Christian doctrine falls apart.
>
> Verses 20-29 – The resurrection is God's plan for victory in the lives of individual Christians as well as for final triumph in the Kingdom of God as a whole.
>
> Verses 30-34 – The entire foundation for the Christian ethic collapses if we lose sight of the resurrection.
>
> Verses 35-50 – Even though it is a concept which is almost impossible to comprehend with only human logic, Paul tried to explain the concept of the identity retained in the resurrection even though there will be a transformation in terms of our material nature.
>
> Verses 51-57 – Paul next explained that not everyone would experience the resurrection because some would short-circuit the system at the time of the Lord's Second Coming, going directly to the transformed state without first experiencing death.
>
> Verse 58 – Paul concluded this section with a challenge to live lives stabilized by their convictions of the coming resurrection.

Prayer Focus: Lord, help me to always view this temporal segment of life in the perspective of life's eternal whole. Amen.
Notes:

Spiritual Journal:

Week: Thirty
Day: Thursday
Book: I Corinthians
Chapter: Sixteen
Memory Verse: Fourteen
Principle: This chapter of individual greetings and personal matters reminds us that the Christian life isn't theology; it really is relationship with God and the members of the community of faith.
Outline:

> Verses 1-4 – Paul encouraged the church concerning the collection for the saints in Jerusalem.
>
> Verses 5-9 – He explained to them his travel plans, which included visiting them.
>
> Verses 10-12 – He asked them to welcome his representatives.
>
> Verses 13-14 – He gave the church a friendly pep talk to keep on in their faith.
>
> Verses 15-18 – He listed a few personal notes concerning friends within the congregation.
>
> Verses 19-24 – He closed the letter with encouragement not only from himself but also from others within the family of faith.

Prayer Focus: Lord, help me to always keep the gospel in flesh and blood, not in libraries and lecture halls. Amen.
Notes:

Spiritual Journal:

Week: Thirty
Day: Friday
Book: II Corinthians
Chapter: One
Memory Verse: Twenty
Principle: Anything we experience as Christians becomes a training course for equipping us to help others through similar difficulties.
Outline:
Verses 1-2 – Paul extended his usual salutation to the church.
Verses 3-14 – He explained that problems he personally, or the church in general, encounters are simply an opportunity to mature in the ability to help others.
Verses 15-16 – He expressed his desire to come personally to visit the church.
Verses 17-24 – Paul expressed a theological truth concerning the surety of God's promises as he explained that he was not double minded in his failing to fulfill his decision to visit them; rather, he wanted to grant them time before his arrival to correct some issues which he had previously addressed.
Prayer Focus: Lord, help me to see not just the silver lining around each dark cloud but to be able to realize that actually there are only dark linings of difficulties around the silver clouds of opportunity You have given me.   Amen.
Notes:

Spiritual Journal:

Week: Thirty-one
Day: Monday
Book: II Corinthians
Chapter: Two
Memory Verse: Fourteen
Principle: There can always be victory in every situation a Christian faces; even the disturbing problem addressed in the first epistle to this church has resulted in the repentance of the offender, and now Paul can encourage the church to begin to actively restore him.
Outline:
> Verses 1-4 – Paul explained in more detail that he had written rather than visited the church because of the grievous nature of his admonition to them; his prayer was that they could see his love as well as his correction in the lines of the letter.
>
> Verses 5-11 – He exhorted them to actively restore the brother who had been at fault with the warning that lack of restoration could allow an opportunity for Satan to enter.
>
> Verses 12-13 – These verses are a personal interjection expressing Paul's private concern when his trusted companion was not present.
>
> Verses 14-16 – He used the illustration of the Roman victory march to express the believer's position of triumph over every enemy and in every situation, expressing that, to the saint, there is a constant smell of victory while, to the sinner, there is a continual stench of defeat.
>
> Verse 17 – Paul reiterated the purity of his motives and actions toward the church.

Prayer Focus: Lord, I understand that, theoretically, You always cause me to triumph; help me to realize it in my daily experience. Amen.
Notes:

Spiritual Journal:

Week: Thirty-one
Day: Tuesday
Book: II Corinthians
Chapter: Three
Memory Verse: Seventeen
Principle: The relationship which God established with men in the Old Testament was certainly a blessing, but our New Testament relationship far exceeds it.
Outline:
> Verses 1-5 – Paul began this section by reminding the church that he didn't need to establish any sort of credibility in order to give them instruction; their very existence constituted his credentials.
>
> Verses 6-16 – He explained that the previous revelation was so spiritually powerful that Moses had to wear a veil to conceal the glory which rested upon him; yet, that limited relationship with and revelation of God was not able to be compared to the unlimited New Testament reality.
>
> Verses 17-18 – The New Testament revelation produces liberty and life rather than bondage and death.

Prayer Focus: Lord, help me to lay aside any attachment I have for the old revelation and grasp hold of the new relationship.   Amen.
Notes:

Spiritual Journal:

Week: Thirty-one
Day: Wednesday
Book: II Corinthians
Chapter: Four
Memory Verse: Eighteen
Principle: Paul had learned to keep his focus on the heaven he was going to rather than on the hell he was going through; this mentality was his key to continuous victory in his Christian life.
Outline:

Verses 1-2 – Paul announced that he had no hidden agenda or ulterior motives in his ministry.

Verses 3-6 – He explained that anyone who could not see the simple gospel message he was presenting must be blinded by the devil.

Verses 7-12 – He described his situation as being one of constant embattlement, but not one in which he received any blows from which he could not bounce back.

Verses 13-15 – Paul opened a window into his inner spiritual life when he described his resilience as being based on his spoken confession of his internal faith in the resurrection power of Christ and his personal destiny as a minister to the churches.

Verses 16-18 – His ultimate source of authority was his determination to focus on what God was doing in and through him – not on what any enemy, physical or spiritual, was doing to him.

Prayer Focus: Lord, make me able to see whatever I have to face as a light affliction in comparison to the heavy weight of glory which You have awaiting me.   Amen.
Notes:

Spiritual Journal:

Week: Thirty-one
Day: Thursday
Book: II Corinthians
Chapter: Five
Memory Verse: Seventeen
Principle: Paul begins this chapter by talking about the transformation which we will experience when we receive our resurrection bodies; however, he concludes it by emphasizing that we have already received an equally important transformation in our spiritual man through the salvation experience.
Outline:
Verses 1-8 – Paul explained a promise that we would have a new body in the resurrection and expressed the truth that believers have a genuine desire to obtain that glorified state.

Verses 9-13 – He expressed his intensity of ministry activity in terms of the judgment seat of Christ before which his works will be examined.

Verses 14-19 – Additionally, he adds that it was the love of Christ which constrained him to so actively pursue the ministry of reconciliation. Understanding the transformation that has taken place in the lives of those who are in Christ, Paul admonished us not to remember a person's former characteristics but to be agents of reconciliation based on the new creature he has become.

Verses 20-21 – One other reason for the mandate of reconciliation is the fact that we have been sent by God as ambassadors which must demonstrate the reconciling character of the One we represent.

Prayer Focus: Lord, help me to see others through Your eyes rather than to remember them as the errant humans they have been. Amen.
Notes:

Spiritual Journal:

Week: Thirty-one
Day: Friday
Book: II Corinthians
Chapter: Six
Memory Verse: Fourteen
Principle: Perhaps a statement which Paul has made in a different context might fit well here when considering the two seemingly unrelated concepts expressed in this chapter: "Bad company corrupts good morals." The beginning of the chapter deals with Paul's source of spiritual strength to overcome all the obstacles he encounters; the end of the chapter suddenly shifts to an admonition not to be unequally yoked with unbelievers. Perhaps he is suggesting that, even though nothing external could destroy him or his faith, being yoked with unbelief could negate his positive attitude.

Outline:

Verses 1-2 – Paul opened this chapter by explaining that the partner with whom he was yoked is God Himself.

Verses 3-10 – He listed the conditions in which he found himself (verses four and five), along with the qualities with which he met these difficulties (verses six and seven), and the resulting victory in the middle of apparent defeat which he experienced (verses eight through ten).

Verses 11-13 – Paul again expressed his sincere heart of ministry toward the congregation.

Verses 14-18 – When he admonished the believers to disentangle themselves from unbelievers, he added an encouragement that God would become their partner just as He had become Paul's.

Prayer Focus: Lord, I want to be partnered with You. Amen.
Notes:

Spiritual Journal:

Week: Thirty-two
Day: Monday
Book: II Corinthians
Chapter: Seven
Memory Verse: Ten
Principle: The repentance and restoration of a wayward brother is reason enough to take the gamble of offense by confronting him directly with his fault.
Outline:

        Verses 1-4 – Paul admits that he was bold in his confrontation of the congregation concerning their errors.

        Verses 5-7 – He also admits that, until Titus arrived with a positive report, he was troubled by the possible negative effects of that confrontation.

        Verses 8-16 – The sorrow which Paul inflicted upon the congregation by confronting them squarely was turned into rejoicing for them in their reconciliation and for the apostle in seeing the restoration of his brothers and because his confidence in the congregation was validated.

Prayer Focus: Lord, help me to care enough about my brother to confront him in genuine loving concern for his restoration. Amen.
Notes:

Spiritual Journal:

Week: Thirty-two
Day: Tuesday
Book: II Corinthians
Chapter: Eight
Memory Verse: Nine
Principle: Sacrificial giving to bless the Body of Christ is patterned after the giving of Jesus Christ Himself who lives in and through believers.
Outline:

> Verses 1-5 – Paul used the Macedonian church as an example of sacrificial giving by saying that they actually gave beyond their ability, begging Paul to receive their offering even though they were in poverty themselves.
>
> Verses 6-7 – Titus was commissioned to encourage the church to be as developed in their giving as they were in all their other spiritual gifts and abilities.
>
> Verses 8-12 – Paul admonished the believers not because he felt spiritually bound to do so but because he wanted to ensure that no one would have legitimate cause to accuse the church of fault in this area.
>
> Verses 13-15 – Paul recognized that the church had abundance and admonished them to be generous to their needy brothers.
>
> Verses 16-23 – Paul commended Titus and his companion as men to be accepted with respect by the church.
>
> Verse 24 – The congregation's offering would be proof of their love and validation of Paul's confidence in the church; in modern terminology, they were to "put their money where their mouth is."

Prayer Focus: Lord, help me to have Your perspective concerning money. Amen.
Notes:

Spiritual Journal:

Week: Thirty-two
Day: Wednesday
Book: II Corinthians
Chapter: Nine
Memory Verse: Eight
Principle: God always sees to it that we receive repayment and increase for everything we give into His Kingdom.
Outline:

        Verses 1-5 – Paul reiterates and recaps all that he had previously said concerning the collection for the saints in Jerusalem.

        Verses 6-15 – Having established the physical background for the offering, Paul turned to the spiritual aspects of giving: God gives back to the one who gives; He repays not only according to the amount given but also according to the attitude in which it was given; He sees to it that a giver will always have resources not only for his personal needs but also for giving into every worthy need; and the act of giving brings glory to God – the Giver of the unspeakable gift of salvation.

Prayer Focus: Lord, thank you for the seed You have placed in my hand; help me to be sensitive and willing when it is time to plant it.   Amen.

Notes:

Spiritual Journal:

Week: Thirty-two
Day: Thursday
Book: II Corinthians
Chapter: Ten
Memory Verse: Four
Principle: A spiritual Christian is equipped with weapons unknown to the natural man; these weapons can actually root out destructive and empty thoughts and mental attitudes which are not after the nature of Christ.
Outline:
> Verses 1-5 – In what almost seems like a warning, Paul encourages the church to deal with any problems before his personal arrival so that he can deal with them meekly rather than having to use the spiritual arsenal against their problems.
>
> Verses 6-11 – He explains that he would rather fire those weapons from a distance by remote control through a letter than to detonate them personally on his visit.
>
> Verses 12-18 – Boasting is one area which must especially be attacked with those powerful spiritual weapons; the only boasting which will remain standing after such an attack will be the bragging we do concerning what Christ has done in our lives.
Prayer Focus: Lord, help me to use that spiritual artillery against my own thought life before I dare to aim it at anyone else.   Amen.
Notes:

Spiritual Journal:

Week: Thirty-two
Day: Friday
Book: II Corinthians
Chapter: Eleven
Memory Verse: Thirty
Principle: The weaknesses and inabilities in our own lives are actually God's open window through which to reveal Himself in us.
Outline:

Verses 1-6 – Paul explains that the discussion he is going to enter into is to make a point concerning his relationship with the church; he is taking this position because he is concerned that they might be moved away from the foundation he has seen laid in their lives.

Verses 7-11 – He explains that in his great love for the church, he denied himself the privilege of receiving a salary from them.

Verses 12-15 – He expresses the idea that Satan was sending his ambassadors in disguise as God's messengers into the church to bring destruction.

Verses 16-20 – He explains that even though he is talking about all that he has done for the church, he is not doing it for the purpose of boasting but to help them see his ministry to them.

Verses 21-33 – He lists the many qualities and activities which should distinguish him from the false messengers as the true apostle to the church.

Prayer Focus: Lord, help me to see You in my weaknesses and to allow You to be seen through my strengths and weaknesses.   Amen.
Notes:

Spiritual Journal:

Week: Thirty-three
Day: Monday
Book: II Corinthians
Chapter: Twelve
Memory Verse: Nine
Principle: Paul's thorn in the flesh has often been the foundation for teachings concerning sufferings which do not align with the rest of the New Testament's revelation. It is important to notice that, although he doesn't tell us who gave him the thorn, he does say that it was a messenger of Satan; this suggests that it was Satan – not God – who sent the thorn. It should also be noticed that the thorn was spoken of as a person rather than a sickness; this suggests that the problem was either a demonic spirit which personally harassed the apostle or a person controlled by such a tormenting spirit. With these thoughts in mind, it becomes clear that Paul's message to us is that God will always give us everything we need in order to deal with anything the devil may dish out.
Outline:
> Verses 1-6 – Paul continued the argument from the previous chapter by listing spiritual visions as another category in which he can be compared with the false messengers.
> Verses 7-13 – Paul confirmed that even in dealing with his thorn in the flesh, his apostleship is confirmed rather than denied.
> Verses 14-21 – Paul announced his desire to visit the church and challenged them to deal with any sins and problems prior to his arrival.
Prayer Focus: Lord, help me to never blame You for any difficulties which I have to deal with in life; rather, help me to realize how You are there in the middle of the situation giving me grace to deal with it. Amen.
Notes:

Spiritual Journal:

Week: Thirty-three
Day: Tuesday
Book: II Corinthians
Chapter: Thirteen
Memory Verse: Eleven
Principle: It is possible to get beyond all the divisions and problems which arise in the community of faith and live together in perfection.
Outline:

> Verses 1-3 – Paul continued with his admonition to prepare themselves for his visit.
>
> Verse 4 – He reminded them of the fact that the crucifixion, although it looked like weakness, was the most powerful event in history.
>
> Verses 5-10 – The apparent weakness of the apostle and of the church can prove to be the strength of God.
>
> Verses 11-12 – He closed the letter with a command – not a suggestion – that the church operate in perfection, unity, and peace.
>
> Verses 13-14 – The closing of the letter incorporated the blessing of the earthly Body of Christ and the individual blessings of the total Trinity.

Prayer Focus: Lord, help me to realize that perfection is not just a target to shoot for but a real bull's eye which can be obtained.   Amen.

Notes:

Spiritual Journal:

Week: Thirty-three

Day: Wednesday

Book: Galatians

Chapter: One

Memory Verse: Eight

Principle: It is easy to get off center and let the essence of the gospel get out of focus; when this happens, heresy comes easily.

Outline:

Verses 1-5 – Paul proclaimed his apostolic authority as he greeted the church.

Verses 6-10 – He expressed his concern that they have moved off center in their understanding of the gospel and proclaimed that any messenger who allowed the essence of the gospel to get out of focus was in truth preaching another gospel and should be judged for heresy.

Verses 11-12 – He claimed that his revelation of the gospel was from direct divine revelation.

Verses 13-24 – Paul shared his testimony of how he was an opponent of the faith until God's predetermined plan that he was to preach the gospel was established; at that point, he retreated to Arabia until he had a clear revelation of the gospel. His message was not influenced by other Christian leaders; he only had brief encounters with them, and those encounters were not until after Paul's message was already solidly formulated.

Prayer Focus: Lord, help me to always keep the heart of the gospel message in sharp focus so that I do not stray into error. Amen.

Notes:

Spiritual Journal:

Week: Thirty-three
Day: Thursday
Book: Galatians
Chapter: Two
Memory Verse: Twenty
Principle: The power of the gospel is in its simplicity: salvation is through faith in Jesus Christ alone; adding any other obligations or regulations perverts, frustrates, and negates it.
Outline:
> Verses 1-10 – Paul referenced the council in Jerusalem when he presented his case and the elders agreed that Christians need not be circumcised.
>
> Verses 11-14 – He also referred to the event in Antioch when Peter and Barnabus wavered in their convictions concerning the simplicity of the salvation message.
>
> Verses 15-18 – Paul presented the logical and theological conclusion that, since trying to earn salvation through good works did not work, the only source of salvation is simple faith in Christ.
>
> Verses 19-21 – The truth of the gospel message is that, because of the new birth, Christ Himself is the one who lives the Christian life through the believer. Any religious efforts on our part only frustrate that operation.

Prayer Focus: Lord, I must admit that I'm a do-it-yourself sort of person; help me to allow You to be the One who does it when it comes to fulfilling the salvation plan in my life.   Amen.
Notes:

Spiritual Journal:

Week: Thirty-three
Day: Friday
Book: Galatians
Chapter: Three
Memory Verse: Twenty-nine

Principle: The Old Testament laws served one simple purpose – to bridge the gap between the giving of the blessing promise under Abraham and the giving of the blessing provision under Christ. To try to use it as the vehicle for the blessing itself is wrong and fruitless.

Outline:

Verses 1-5 – Paul challenged the church over having begun their salvation in faith and then reverted to following the Law.

Verses 6-9 – He demonstrated that our blessing stands on the foundation of Abraham's faith.

Verses 10-12 – Rather than being the foundation of blessing, the Law actually became a source of cursing.

Verses 13-14 – The curse of obligation to fulfill the regulations of the Law was removed by Christ.

Verses 15-25 – He explained that the Law was to serve as a tutor to take the believer through the transition between Abraham and Christ.

Verses 26-29 – All who are in Christ – regardless of race, creed, color, or national origin – are beneficiaries of the blessing through faith.

Prayer Focus: Lord, it is too easy to think that I should be earning Your blessings; help me to really live by faith. Amen.

Notes:

Spiritual Journal:

Week: Thirty-four
Day: Monday
Book: Galatians
Chapter: Four
Memory Verse: Seven
Principle: We have an inheritance in the family of God into which we have been born through the new birth; we are heirs with full rights and privileges – not orphans, illegitimates, guests, or household servants.
Outline:

> Verses 1-7 – Paul used the comparison between heirs and servants to illustrate the point that, in the new birth, we have received the testimony of the Holy Spirit and have the full rights of heirs.

> Verses 8-11 – Prior to their conversion, the members of the congregation served pagan gods and were in bondage to rituals; Paul warned them about slipping back into that kind of servitude.

> Verses 12-16 – Paul questioned what had happened in their relationship with him in that they had so readily received him and his gospel at first but had now drawn back.

> Verses 17-20 – Paul contrasted himself with the teachers who were presently influencing the church – they were zealous, but not beneficial; even though he was not physically present, he was spiritually zealous over their well-being. He was motivated for their good, not for a hidden agenda as was the case with his opponents.

> Verses 21-31 – The analogy of Abraham's two sons illustrated the difference between trying to receive God's blessing by faith and attempting to claim it illegitimately.

Prayer Focus: Lord, the whole idea of getting something for nothing is so foreign to my thinking; help me to see myself as Your heir and to realize what a wonderful plan You have for me. Amen.

Notes:

Spiritual Journal:

Week: Thirty-four

Day: Tuesday

Book: Galatians

Chapter: Five

Memory Verse: Sixteen

Principle: The big problem with the plan of salvation which eliminates our obligation to fulfill the Law is that we too often revert to following the lusts of the flesh; to overcome this tendency, we must learn to walk in the Spirit.

Outline:

Verses 1-6 – Paul explained that we must make an effort to stand in the freedoms of grace; slipping back into thinking that we must keep the Law constitutes falling from the blessing of grace.

Verses 7-12 – Paul focused the problem on the individuals who led the congregation away from walking by faith, saying that they were causing trouble and should be judged.

Verses 13-15 – Yielding to the flesh once you have been freed from the restrictions of the Law is destructive; on the other hand, living by the rule of love will actually fulfill all the objectives behind the ordinances of the Law.

Verses 16-18 – The only way to win the battle against the operations of the flesh is to live having your spirit man empowered by the Holy Spirit.

Verses 19-23 – When Paul contrasted the results of living according to flesh with the results of living after the spirit, he made the difference even more obvious by calling the fleshly activities "works" and the spiritual qualities "fruit."

Verses 24-26 – He concluded that it is mandatory to eliminate the flesh's control and accentuate the spirit's control.

Prayer Focus: Lord, I want to walk according to the Holy Spirit's direction in my human spirit; help me to be more sensitive to Your leading. Amen.

Notes:

Spiritual Journal:

Week: Thirty-four
Day: Wednesday
Book: Galatians
Chapter: Six
Memory Verse: Eight
Principle: Every action and attitude will produce a result – good or bad – depending on
whether the motivation comes from the spirit or the flesh.
Outline:

Verses 1-6 – In answer to the question posed by Cain, yes, we are our brother's
keeper; we must help him when he errs. At the same time, we must be
circumspect concerning our own possibility of erring.

Verses 7-10 – Since every action and attitude will produce a harvest in
accordance with the nature of the seed we plant, Paul admonished the
congregation to be careful not to slack off on their good deeds.

Verse 11 – Paul affirmed that this message was so important that he wrote it in a
personal letter with his own hand; likely, the marking was heavy because
of prison chains on his wrist or perhaps due to poor lighting in his cell.

Verses 12-14 – He contrasted the motive of his ministry to them with that of the
so-called ministry they were receiving from others.

Verses 15-18 – He ended the letter with a positive note of encouragement to the
believers.

Prayer Focus: Lord, to walk in the spirit is my biggest need.   Amen.
Notes:

Spiritual Journal:

Week: Thirty-four
Day: Thursday
Book: Ephesians
Chapter: One
Memory Verse: Eighteen
Principle: Unless God divinely reveals His abundant blessings to us, we have no way of actually comprehending all that He has in store for us.
Outline:

Verses 1-2 – In the greeting, Paul identified himself and his apostleship and offered a blessing to the believers.

Verses 3-6 – He explained that God has a predetermined plan to abundantly bless the believers.

Verses 7-10 – He expounded that our redemption is not just salvation, but an abounding blessing which can be a mystery unless His will is revealed to us.

Verses 11-12 – The blessings of our inheritance are to bring glory to God.

Verses 13-14 – The indwelling Holy Spirit is the down payment on the great promises in store for the believer.

Verses 15-23 – Paul prayed that the church would have supernatural revelation of what exactly God has provided for them through the resurrection and exaltation of Jesus Christ.

Prayer Focus: Lord, I don't want to miss out on Your exceedingly great and abundant promises; open my spiritual eyes to realize what You have provided for me. Amen.

Notes:

Spiritual Journal:

Week: Thirty-five

Day: Friday

Book: Ephesians

Chapter: Two

Memory Verse: Eight

Principle: Even though we were totally unworthy, Christ Jesus has given us not only salvation but also unspeakable riches and authority.

Outline:

        Verses 1-3 – We have been raised to a position of authority above all the forces of hell which once ruled over us.

        Verses 4-7 – We have been positioned so that God can manifest the exceeding riches of His great grace in us.

        Verses 8-10 – These blessings are not due to our earning them but are entirely dependent upon God's predetermined plan of blessing.

        Verses 11-19 – In this redemption, God has brought together the Jew and the gentile who were alienated from one another as well as from Him.

        Verses 20-22 – We are now built together into the church of God.

Prayer Focus: Lord, I want to be the kind of person that does indeed show forth the praise and glory of God; help me to fully appropriate Your promises.   Amen.

Notes:

Spiritual Journal:

Week: Thirty-five
Day: Monday
Book: Ephesians
Chapter: Three
Memory Verse: Seventeen
Principle: The church's comprehension of and acquisition of God's promises through His love becomes a message to the demonic world of God's great plan and wisdom.
Outline:
>   Verses 1-9 – Paul established the fact (which was not understood in previous generations) that God's plan of including the gentiles in His plan of salvation has now been supernaturally revealed to the apostles and prophets.
>
>   Verses 10-12 – One intention of the exaltation of the church is to prove to the demonic realm that God has a good plan for man and that He is able to fulfill it.
>
>   Verses 13-21 – Paul prayed for the church that they would experience the love of God, which is actually beyond human comprehension, and that it would establish them even during times of tribulation.

Prayer Focus: Lord, how can I know the unknowable? How can I experience Your four-dimensional love in our three-dimensional world? Help me. Amen.
Notes:

Spiritual Journal:

Week: Thirty-five
Day: Tuesday
Book: Ephesians
Chapter: Four
Memory Verse: Thirty

Principle: Having seen the place of exaltation to which we have been called, it is our awesome responsibility to see that we walk worthy of that calling.

Outline:

Verses 1-2 – Paul laid out a mandate that we walk worthy of all the plan of God which had been predetermined for us.

Verses 3-6 – The first area of proving our worthiness is in establishing peace and unity within the fellowship of faith.

Verses 7-11 – Recognizing and functioning under the leadership of the five-fold ministry is a major key to church unity.

Verses 12-16 – Paul set forth the purpose and end result of having such leadership established in the church.

Verses 17-24 – He contrasted the unregenerate mindset of the unbeliever with the renewed mentality of the believer.

Verses 25-32 – Next, he spelled out some of the practical steps to follow in demonstrating a life worthy of its calling.

Prayer Focus: Lord, I know that I need a lot of help in living up to the quality of life You have predestined for me; in fact, I realize that I actually need You to live that life through me. Amen.

Notes:

Spiritual Journal:

Week: Thirty-five

Day: Wednesday

Book: Ephesians

Chapter: Five

Memory Verse: One

Principle: Our spiritual advancement can be easily measured by our relationships in the home, on the job, and in society.

Outline:

       Verses 1-2 – Our walk with God is a walk of love with our fellowman.

       Verses 3-13 – It is also a walk that demands purity and deliberate separation from the evil we once participated in.

       Verses 14-21 – It is a proactive walk of vigilance.

       Verses 22-33 – The relationship within our marriage mirrors the relationship we have with the Lord.

Prayer Focus: Lord, help me to realize that the way I relate to others is a window into the relationship I have with You. Amen.

Notes:

Spiritual Journal:

Week: Thirty-five
Day: Thursday
Book: Ephesians
Chapter: Six
Memory Verse: Ten
Principle: Seen from God's perspective, any difficulties we have are not with the humans we deal with but with demonic forces which are using them as pawns in a struggle against us.
Outline:
> Verses 1-4 – Paul continued his instruction from the previous chapter by showing us that our Christian walk is demonstrated by our relationships with our children and parents.
>
> Verses 5-9 – Our Christian walk is also demonstrated in our relationships at the workplace.
>
> Verses 10-17 – Concerning our confrontation with the demonic forces, it is important to note that Paul's emphasis is on standing, not on fighting. The term he used is one of holding a victorious position. In other words, if we arm ourselves with the proper spiritual attire, we are positioned in authority whenever the enemy tries to confront us.
>
> Verses 18-20 – Our real battle with the enemy is when we attack him through our prayers.
>
> Verses 21-24 – Paul closed the letter with a personal note and a word of encouragement.

Prayer Focus: Lord, help me to never surrender my position of authority where You have invited me to sit with You in the heavenly places far above all other spiritual powers. Amen.
Notes:

Spiritual Journal:

Week: Thirty-five
Day: Friday
Book: Philippians
Chapter: One
Memory Verse: Twenty-one

Principle: Paul stated that God was determined to complete whatever purpose He had begun in the believers' lives. He would preserve Paul's life even as he faced possible execution for one simple reason: God's purpose is the foundation and source of meaning for our lives.

Outline:

Verses 1-5 – Paul opened the letter with an introduction, a greeting, a prayer, and a thanksgiving.

Verses 6-7 – He followed with an encouragement that God's purposes were being fulfilled in the believers.

Verses 8-11 – He prayed for increase of spiritual blessings in their lives.

Verses 12-19 – Paul encouraged the believers with his expectancy that God's good purposes were being worked out in his life even though he was in prison and some were using his imprisonment as an occasion to vent their envy and strife.

Verses 20-24 – Facing possible execution, Paul expressed his willingness to fulfill the purpose of God in his dying or living – he personally preferred to go on to be with the Lord but was willing to remain as long as he could minister to the saints.

Verses 25-26 – He concluded that it was likely the purpose of God for him to remain alive for the benefit of the Body of Christ.

Verses 27-30 – He challenged the church that their lifestyle should be in alignment with the gospel of Christ, even as they faced opposition.

Prayer Focus: Lord, help me to become totally convinced that Your purpose is being worked out in my life and help me live accordingly. Amen.

Notes:

Spiritual Journal:

Week: Thirty-six
Day: Monday
Book: Philippians
Chapter: Two
Memory Verse: Five

Principle: Not only through the theology of the life of Christ but also through the testimonies of the lives of Timothy and Epaphroditus, Paul presented the principle of self-sacrifice for the benefit of others.

Outline:

Verses 1-4 – Paul elaborated on the idea that hearing that the church was living lives of selflessness was the source of his fulfillment and joy.

Verses 5-8 – He admonished the believers to have the same self-sacrificing mentality that Christ had when He willingly gave up His position with God to redeem mankind.

Verses 9-11 – Paul added that Jesus' sacrifice resulted in His exaltation.

Verses 12-18 – He listed a few of the benefits which they will receive as a result of their self-giving.

Verses 19-24 – Timothy was presented as a classic example of the true Christian who willingly gives himself for others.

Verses 25-30 – Epaphroditus is also a sterling example of Christian selflessness.

Prayer Focus: Lord, it is too easy to have a self-centered mental attitude. Help me to obtain and maintain the mindset of Christ. Amen.

Notes:

Spiritual Journal:

Week: Thirty-six
Day: Tuesday
Book: Philippians
Chapter: Three
Memory Verse: Eight

Principle: There is nothing of value in our human qualifications; all that counts in our lives is what God has done in us.

Outline:

Verses 1-4 – Paul warned the church to be cautious of those who would try to depend upon human qualifications.

Verses 5-8 – He advanced the idea that if anyone could depend upon his personal qualifications, it would be himself; yet, he considered his qualifications and accomplishments as totally valueless.

Verses 9-14 – He explained that, even though he had not achieved the place in Christ that he was aiming for, he continued to strive for that place – knowing that only there would his life have meaning.

Verses 15-19 – Paul challenged the church to strive for this quality of Christ-mindedness and to take careful note of those who thought and acted in opposition.

Verses 20-21 – He encouraged them that Christ will bring about a metamorphosis in them.

Prayer Focus: Lord, help me to always see that, even if I seem perfect by human standards, I am still worthless except that You are transforming me and working Your character into me. Amen.

Notes:

Spiritual Journal:

Week: Thirty-six
Day: Wednesday
Book: Philippians
Chapter: Four
Memory Verse: Eight
Principle: Always looking for the good in every person and in each situation is a key to a
      fulfilled and fulfilling life.
Outline:
> Verses 1-3 – Paul's personal comments to individuals in the church demonstrated
> that his teachings were not just good philosophies but were practical life
> principles to be put into actual operation.
>
> Verses 4-7 – Paul listed a number of positive life qualities which result in having
> the peace of God ruling in our lives.
>
> Verses 8-9 – Next, he added one final life quality which results in having not only
> the peace of God, but also the God of peace Himself.
>
> Verses 10-19 – Paul concluded his letter with a note concerning the financial gift
> they had sent to him. Although it is personal in nature, the message
> contains some beneficial teachings concerning the principles of giving,
> with the main emphasis on the fact that Paul was not interested in his
> personal gain from their giving but rather in the benefit that the church
> would receive from their act of selflessness: God would see that all their
> needs were also met in abundance.
>
> Verses 20-23 – He concluded the letter with a blessing and a greeting from the
> saints.

Prayer Focus: Lord, help me to always see, think, and believe the best concerning each
      person and in every situation; help me to always recognize that the glass truly is
      half full – not half empty. Amen.
Notes:

Spiritual Journal:

Week: Thirty-six
Day: Thursday
Book: Colossians
Chapter: One
Memory Verse: Thirteen
Principle: The work of God in our lives is two-fold: we are translated out of the kingdom
of darkness and translated into the Kingdom of God.
Outline:
Verses 1-8 – Paul opened this letter with an identification of himself, an address
to the saints, a thanksgiving for their testimony, and a commendation for
their faith.
Verses 9-11 – He prayed for their spiritual growth.
Verses 12-19 – Paul used what seems to be an existing hymn to express the
qualities and attributes of Christ:
a) Deliverer
b) Redeemer
c) God's image
d) Creator
e) Pre-existent One
f) Purpose for all existence
g) Head of the church
h) Embodiment of all fullness
Verses 20-29 – He described the mystery of the redemptive work of the cross but
added the need for the believer to participate in that redemptive process.
Prayer Focus: Lord, help me to have a revelation of who You really are so that I can truly
receive the fullness of Your redemptive process in my life.   Amen.
Notes:

Spiritual Journal:

Week: Thirty-six
Day: Friday
Book: Colossians
Chapter: Two
Memory Verse: Fourteen
Principle: We must learn to be cautious of religious sounding teachings and pious-looking rituals; they may be traps to pull us away from the simplicity of a simple relationship with Christ.

Outline:

Verses 1-3 – Paul's statement concerning his desire for the believers to understand the hidden wisdom and knowledge of God stands in contrast to the mystic teachings by which others will desire that they be fooled.

Verses 4-7 – He encouraged them to be rooted in the faith so that they will not be fooled by deceptive teachings.

Verses 8-10 – He warned them to hold to their relationship with Christ to protect them from being polluted with deceiving thoughts.

Verses 11-17 – He expressed the power of the baptism as a definitive eradication of condemnation from the believer.

Verses 18-23 – He challenged the church to be cautious not to allow anyone to influence them into returning to the bondage of serving the elements from which Christ has set them free.

Prayer Focus: Lord, help me to be so full of Your Word that I will automatically live above being fooled by men's doctrines.   Amen.

Notes:

Spiritual Journal:

Week: Thirty-seven
Day: Monday
Book: Colossians
Chapter: Three
Memory Verse: Seventeen
Principle: It has been said of some people that they are too heavenly minded to be of any earthly good; however, this chapter teaches us that being heavenly minded (seeking those things which are above) will show in the earthly relationships we have (husband-wife, parent-child, and employer-employee).
Outline:
>Verses 1-7 – Paul used the sacrament of baptism to illustrate the principle that the believer has actually died to the present world system and has been raised to a new life in Christ. The result is that he should constantly make sure that worldly impulses, attitudes, and actions are determined dead and void while the believer lives with an active focus on heavenly realities.

>Verses 8-14 – Next, to further illustrate the change that takes place in a believer's life, Paul turned to one particular aspect of the ancient baptism ritual: the practice of taking off the worn and dirty coat and replacing it with a clean new one as the convert came up out of the waters of baptism. Paul listed a number of old qualities which were to be discarded like the old garment and a number of new qualities to be acquired.

>Verses 15-17 – He clarified the point that the attributes of the Kingdom of God will not automatically appear in a person's life; he has to will to let them dwell and rule in him.

>Verses 18-25 – Human relations are true indicators of our spiritual relationship.

Prayer Focus: Lord, I have long since dried off from my physical baptism; let me always remain soaking wet with the baptismal realities in the spiritual dimension. Amen.
Notes:

Spiritual Journal:

Week: Thirty-seven
Day: Tuesday
Book: Colossians
Chapter: Four
Memory Verse: Six
Principle: Say, pray, stray – three important principles (how we pray, how we walk or conduct ourselves, and how we talk and present our faith) seem to sum up the focus of the Christian life.
Outline:
> Verse 1 – Paul carried over a point concerning employer-employee relationships from the previous chapter.
>
> Verses 2-6 – Three very crucial areas of the Christian life (prayer, conduct, and language) were reemphasized as Paul concluded the epistle.
>
> Verses 7-18 – Personal notes to and concerning individuals within the church established the point that the gospel is not simply philosophy – it is real flesh-and-blood living.

Prayer Focus: Lord, it is easy to let the gospel concepts remain principle rather than practice; help me to walk the walk as well as to talk the talk.   Amen.
Notes:

Spiritual Journal:

Week: Thirty-seven
Day: Wednesday
Book: I Thessalonians
Chapter: One
Memory Verse: Six
Principle: The testimony of faith – especially faith under fire – is a true Christian's seal of approval.
Outline:

Verses 1-2 – Paul opened his letter with a greeting and a thanksgiving.

Verses 3-4 – He added a commendation for their testimony.

Verse 5 – He reminded them of the nature – both spiritual and moral – of his ministry to them.

Verses 6-10 – Paul confirmed that the believers had established an example and a testimony which had brought results in the lives of other believers who encountered them.

Prayer Focus: Lord, help me to live a life that is noticed by others and brings about noticeable change in them. Amen.
Notes:

Spiritual Journal:

Week: Thirty-seven
Day: Thursday
Book: I Thessalonians
Chapter: Two
Memory Verse: Thirteen
Principle: The fullest joy a believer can experience is to see those he has led to the Lord and mentored become exemplary Christians.
Outline:

Verses 1-12 – Paul described the demeanor in which he ministered to the church:

a) Without deceit
b) Without uncleanness
c) Without guile
d) Without flattery
e) Without covetousness
f) Without desire for prestige
g) With gentleness
h) With self-sacrifice
i) With lowly, just, and blameless behavior
j) With fatherly care

Verse 13 – He was thankful for the effectual results of his ministry in their lives.

Verses 14-18 – Having discussed the difficulties experienced universally in the church (in himself, in the gentile church, and in the Jewish church), Paul concluded that these difficulties were Satan's own work.

Verses 19-20 – He confirmed that the saints themselves were his reward in the ministry.

Prayer Focus: Lord, help me live so that those who ministered to me can consider me to be a trophy of their ministry, and help me to minister to others with the quality of ministry which will produce disciples whom I can consider trophies.   Amen.

Notes:

Spiritual Journal:

Week: Thirty-seven
Day: Friday
Book: I Thessalonians
Chapter: Three
Memory Verse: Eight
Principle: In our human nature, we often come to the place where we can no longer forbear; at these times, a word of encouragement can make the difference between life and death. At all times, our faith is the sustaining force in our lives.
Outline:

> Verses 1-8 – Paul described how, when he was at the very limit of his emotional resources, the testimony from the believers encouraged him and renewed his ability to stand.
> Verses 9-13 – Paul's prayers for the church were twofold: thanks and intercession.

Prayer Focus: Lord, help my testimony and prayers to be an encouragement to others and send others with testimonies of encouragement across my path at the crucial moments of my life. Amen.
Notes:

Spiritual Journal:

Week: Thirty-eight
Day: Monday
Book: I Thessalonians
Chapter: Four
Memory Verse: Sixteen
Principle: Even though this chapter deals with two distinctly separate topics, they can be seen together in that our perspective on the afterlife is foundational for our ability to live properly in the present.
Outline:
Verses 1-12 – Paul admonished the church to live to please the Lord:
a) Morally
b) Spiritually
c) Academically
d) Financially
Verses 13-18 – He also addressed the afterlife:
a) The dead will be raised prior to the translation of the living saints.
b) The living saints will be caught up at the sound of the last trumpet.
c) We will be with the Lord forever after this translation.
d) This truth should be a source of comfort.
Prayer Focus: Lord, help me to live my life with two worlds in constant view: the present one in which I must live worthy of You and the coming one where I will live eternally with You. Amen.
Notes:

Spiritual Journal:

Week: Thirty-eight
Day: Tuesday
Book: I Thessalonians
Chapter: Five
Memory Verse: Twenty-three
Principle: As a tri-partite creation consisting of body, soul, and spirit, we must serve the Lord on three different levels of reality.
Outline:

Verses 1-8 – Paul discussed the timing of the coming of the Lord and concluded that the important issue wasn't the timing itself but the fact that, as children of the light, we are ready always.

Verses 9-11 – The fact that we can be ready for the Lord's coming, whether we live to see it or not, is a source of comfort to us.

Verses 12-22 – Paul set forth some simple rules for living ready for the Lord's coming:

a) Respect the Christian leadership
b) Exhort those who need encouragement
c) Warn the unruly
d) Comfort the distressed
e) Support the weak
f) Be patient with everyone
g) Rejoice
h) Pray
i) Be thankful
j) Do not quench the Spirit
k) Confirm the good
l) Disdain evil

Verses 23-24 – Even though he had listed so many obligations for the believer, Paul concluded that it was really not the believer himself but God who would do the work through the believer.

Verses 25-28 – He closed his letter with a blessing for the congregation.

Prayer Focus: Lord, help me to totally yield my entire self (body, soul, and spirit) to You. Amen.

Notes:

Spiritual Journal:

Week: Thirty-eight
Day: Wednesday
Book: II Thessalonians
Chapter: One
Memory Verse: Twelve
Principle: The victories in our Christian lives produce two great results: they cause Christ to be glorified in us and us to be glorified in Christ.
Outline:
        Verses 1-4 – Paul opened the letter with a blessing and a thanksgiving for the congregation's testimony of faith and patience.
        Verses 5-6 – Their testimony was proof of God's righteous judgment.
        Verses 7-10 – Ultimate vindication is promised at the return of Christ.
        Verses 11-12 – Paul prayed that they would remain worthy of this recompense and that God would be glorified in them and they in Him.
Prayer Focus: Lord, help me to not only live up to the standard required for me to be glorified in You, but, more importantly, to live so that You can be glorified in me. Amen.
Notes:

Spiritual Journal:

Week: Thirty-eight

Day: Thursday

Book: II Thessalonians

Chapter: Two

Memory Verse: Eight

Principle: God has predetermined plans for all of creation: to consume the wicked and to exalt the righteous.

Outline:

Verses 1-2 – Paul addressed the issue of confusion concerning the timing of the coming of the Lord which had apparently resulted from falsified letters bearing Paul's name.

Verses 3-5 – He reminded them of two basic factors which he had already determined must be in place before the return of the Lord: apostasy and the appearance of the man of sin.

Verses 6-8 – He affirmed that the present church was holding back the appearance of this wicked one and that, once he does appear, God will judge him.

Verses 9-14 – Paul contrasted those who would submit themselves to following this wicked one and the righteous who are called to follow the Lord.

Verses 15-17 – He encouraged them to stand in faith and prayed that Jesus, who had already blessed them, would establish them in all good works and words.

Prayer Focus: Lord, as we see the evil day approaching, help me to keep my focus on You rather than on the evil one who is trying to establish himself. Amen.

Notes:

Spiritual Journal:

Week: Thirty-eight
Day: Friday
Book: II Thessalonians
Chapter: Three
Memory Verse: Five
Principle: Purging within the church as a whole is as important as purging within the individual believer.
Outline:

>> Verses 1-2 – Paul asked for the church's intercession on his behalf.
>>
>> Verses 3-5 – He encouraged the church concerning his confidence that, because of His faithfulness, God was doing what was best for the church.
>>
>> Verses 6-15 – He drew upon the long-standing example of his own life and practice as he instructed the believers to separate from unrighteousness in the congregation.
>>
>> Verses 16-18 – He closed the letter with a blessing and encouragement.

Prayer Focus: Lord, help me to be discerning about evil that is within and around me, but more importantly, to be aware of Your great faithfulness to establish Your good plan and purpose in my life.   Amen.

Notes:

Spiritual Journal:

Week: Thirty-nine
Day: Monday
Book: I Timothy
Chapter: One
Memory Verse: Nineteen
Principle: Our faith in and relationship with Christ are treasures to be guarded lest they be corrupted and lost.
Outline:

 Verses 1-2 – Paul opened the letter with his traditional greeting and blessing.

 Verses 3-4 – He identified Timothy's assignment of preventing the congregation from corrupting their faith.

 Verses 5-11 – He explained that the New Testament commandments differed from the Old Testament Law; the New Testament commandments are directives for displaying love and a good conscience rather than a corrective for those with evil motives.

 Verses 12-17 – Paul used his own testimony to illustrate the transforming power of the gospel.

 Verses 18-20 – He encouraged Timothy to aggressively defend his relationship with Christ in light of the experiences of others whose faith had been destroyed.

Prayer Focus: Lord, help me to steer a safe course of faith and conduct, avoiding the treacheries of heresy and rebellion which would shipwreck my spiritual life. Amen.

Notes:

Spiritual Journal:

Week: Thirty-nine
Day: Tuesday
Book: I Timothy
Chapter: Two
Memory Verse: One
Principle: A lifestyle of simple faith and conduct is pleasing to God.
Outline:

> Verses 1-7 – On the basis of God's desire for all men – Jew and gentile – to be saved, Paul exhorted Timothy to pray for all men, especially those in authority.
>
> Verses 8-10 – He expressed a desire for men and women to live lives characterized by sincere simplicity and unpretentious faith.
>
> Verses 11-15 – What Paul said concerning the issue of the position of women in church leadership is often misunderstood. He actually advanced the role of women by offering them the opportunity to learn – an opportunity not commonly available in the contemporary culture. His statements concerning the woman's usurping authority over a man are actually based on the individual husband-wife relationship rather than the general male-female issue. His teaching concerning Adam and Eve is related to the fact that, in Genesis 2:17, God commanded Adam not to eat of the Tree of the Knowledge of Good and Evil, but He did not create Eve until verse 21. It was Adam's responsibility to avoid the tree, but Eve overruled his authority. However, it was through Eve that salvation came into the world (Genesis 3:15) and sin is counted through Adam (Romans 5:12).

Prayer Focus: Lord, it is so easy to get caught up in too many peripheral ideas and activities; help me to hold to the simplicity of faith and conduct which pleases You. Amen.

Notes:

Spiritual Journal:

Week: Thirty-nine
Day: Wednesday
Book: I Timothy
Chapter: Three
Memory Verse: Sixteen
Principle: The mystery of godliness – the incarnation – demands moral quality in church leadership because leaders, too, are required to manifest God in human flesh.
Outline:

Verses 1-7 – The qualities of a bishop include:
a) Family life
b) Personal habits and attitudes
c) Reputation in the community
d) Stability in the church

Verses 8-13 – Deacons must qualify along the same lines.

Verses 14-15 – Paul expressed his desire to personally come to be with Timothy, but challenged him to keep a high standard even if the visit was delayed.

Verse 16 – The mystery of Christ's incarnation is the foundation for our standards and conduct.

Prayer Focus: Lord, help me to live up to Your standard even if I'm not a bishop or deacon. Amen.
Notes:

Spiritual Journal:

Week: Thirty-nine
Day: Thursday
Book: I Timothy
Chapter: Four
Memory Verse: One
Principle: Because there are seducing spirits which desire to draw us away from the faith, it is imperative that believers pay close attention to their personal conduct and doctrine.
Outline:

Verses 1-5 – The Holy Spirit warned the church that demonic spirits would work to draw believers away from sound doctrine to perverted heresies.

Verses 6-11 – Paul challenged Timothy to teach the believers to carefully nourish themselves with sound doctrine and spiritual exercise.

Verses 12-16 – He encouraged Timothy in his personal ministry; in spite of his youthfulness, Timothy should:

a) Demonstrate an exemplary life

b) Focus on sound doctrine

c) Activate the spiritual gifts

d) Concentrate totally on his personal conduct and teaching

Prayer Focus: Lord, help me to live circumspectly and intently in light of the deception around me.   Amen.
Notes:

Spiritual Journal:

Week: Thirty-nine
Day: Friday
Book: I Timothy
Chapter: Five
Memory Verse: Eighteen
Principle: True elders within the Body of Christ deserve proper respect.
Outline:

> Verses 1-2 – Paul required proper respect for elderly members of the congregation.
>
> Verses 3-16 – He outlined the obligations of the church toward widows:
>> a) Let their relatives care for them if possible.
>>
>> b) Church support should not go to younger women or ones with questionable testimonies.
>>
>> c) Let those who are able to remarry do so.
>
> Verses 17-18 – Financial support for elders is deserved and expected.
>
> Verses 19-21 – Elders in error are to be corrected but only under the proper, carefully controlled conditions.
>
> Verses 22-25 – Be cautious and take plenty of time when ordaining leadership, since some men's qualities and faults do not show up immediately. Verse twenty-three seems to be a personal note which has been jotted here out of context. Its point is often misunderstood as a license for Christians to drink wine; rather, it is a statement concerning the medicinal value of alcohol. Paul is no more encouraging casual drinking than he would have encouraged the non-medicinal use of morphine.

Prayer Focus: Lord, help me to recognize and properly respect those who deserve spiritual honor. Amen.

Notes:

Spiritual Journal:

Week: Forty
Day: Monday
Book: I Timothy
Chapter: Six
Memory Verse: Ten
Principle: In labor-management relationships, in our attitudes toward and use of money, and in our personal goals and ambitions in life, it is important to focus on the fact that the one true treasure we have is our faith in and relationship with Christ.
Outline:

        Verses 1-2 – Proper respect for one's employer is demanded.

        Verses 3-11 – Paul explained that some people feel they can use the gospel as a means to obtain wealth but that such an attitude is in error and can lead to sin and sorrow.

        Verses 12-16 – He encouraged Timothy to flee from such an attitude and to chase after a Christ-like mentality and lifestyle.

        Verses 17-19 – The proper attitude toward wealth is to recognize that it is an uncertain source but a tool given by our true Source (God Himself) for us to enjoy and for us to do good deeds for others.

        Verses 20-21 – Paul ended with a final warning to guard the true treasure – our faith.

Prayer Focus: Lord, help me to recognize the true treasure I have and to properly use my temporal treasures. Amen.
Notes:

Spiritual Journal:

Week: Forty

Day: Tuesday

Book: II Timothy

Chapter: One

Memory Verse: Six

Principle: Although we often speak of "our personal faith," our relationship with God also unites us in a community of faith that includes a heritage from past believers and a responsibility to contemporary ones.

Outline:

Verses 1-2 – Paul's greeting shows his relationship to Timothy.

Verses 3-5 – His thanksgiving mentions his own personal spiritual heritage as well as Timothy's.

Verses 6-7 – Even the anointing of the Holy Spirit on Timothy's life is linked to his relationship to Paul through the laying on of his hands.

Verses 8-12 – The responsibility to support one another is a result of our inter-relationships.

Verses 13-18 – Paul listed some who failed and some who succeeded in supporting their Christian brothers.

Prayer Focus: Lord, help me to stand true not only to You but also to the members of Your Body. Amen.

Notes:

Spiritual Journal:

Week: Forty
Day: Wednesday
Book: II Timothy
Chapter: Two
Memory Verse: Fifteen
Principle: "Keep the main thing the main thing" is a little slogan which might sum up what Paul was saying in this chapter as he admonished Timothy to teach his followers to focus on the major issues of doctrine and conduct while avoiding side issues.
Outline:

Verses 1-2 – Paul told Timothy to keep the gospel advancing by teaching ones who will also teach others.

Verses 3-6 – Using illustrations from everyday life, Paul emphasized the point that people become successful by focusing on their individual assignments.

Verses 7-13 – The core doctrines of the gospel are reiterated as Timothy's area of focus.

Verses 14-26 – Paul charged Timothy to remind his hearers of these things and to instruct them to purify their lives and live as good servants of the Lord.

Prayer Focus: Lord, help me to focus on the main thing and not to "sweat the small stuff." Amen.
Notes:

Spiritual Journal:

Week: Forty
Day: Thursday
Book: II Timothy
Chapter: Three
Memory Verse: Sixteen
Principle: Even in the worst of times, there is one sure source of stability – the Word of
God.
Outline:

Verses 1-9 – Paul prophesied concerning the wicked conditions which will prevail
in the hearts of men in the last days.

Verses 10-17 – He explained that the only preventative medicine and curative
therapy for such conditions is to remain faithful to the truths of the Word
of God.

Prayer Focus: Lord, help me to always keep Your Word before my eyes and to meditate
on it continually and to never let it depart from my mouth; I want to hide it in my
heart so that I will not sin against You.   Amen.
Notes:

Spiritual Journal:

Week: Forty
Day: Friday
Book: II Timothy
Chapter: Four
Memory Verse: Eight
Principle: Even though some will turn to apostasy, for believers the preaching of and believing in the gospel will secure eternal reward.
Outline:
> Verses 1-5 – Although others may turn to false ideas, Timothy is admonished to continue preaching the truth.
>
> Verses 6-8 – Paul gives his own life as an example of the reward awaiting those who remain true to the gospel.
>
> Verses 9-22 – The personal notes in Paul's conclusion reiterate the focus of the letter: that the Body of Christ must support one another and testify of God's faithfulness to His witnesses.

Prayer Focus: Lord, help me to stay true to You and receive the crown of righteousness You have prepared for me.   Amen.
Notes:

Spiritual Journal:

Week: Forty-one
Day: Monday
Book: Titus
Chapter: One
Memory Verse: Fifteen
Principle: True spiritual leadership is necessary to protect the church from error.
Outline:

> Verses 1-4 – In his greeting to Titus, Paul introduced the theme of the letter by associating the power of the gospel with the purity of godliness.
>
> Verses 5-9 – He listed the qualities of a true spiritual leader; these include not only doctrinal purity but also moral and social excellence.
>
> Verses 10-16 – He outlined the danger of false leaders who corrupt the gospel and pollute their followers.

Prayer Focus: Lord, help me always to recognize the right leaders to follow, help correct the false leaders I meet, and properly lead any who may follow me.   Amen.
Notes:

Spiritual Journal:

Week: Forty-one
Day: Tuesday
Book: Titus
Chapter: Two
Memory Verse: Eleven
Principle: Good doctrine must be accompanied with a proper lifestyle.
Outline:

> Verse 1 – Paul admonished Titus to instruct the congregation to live lives that measure up to the quality of the gospel they hold.
>
> Verses 2-8 – Older men and women are to set an example to be followed by the younger generation.
>
> Verses 9-10 – Servants are to live and work honestly.
>
> Verses 11-14 – The redemptive grace of God demands that we eschew evil and espouse righteousness.
>
> Verse 15 – Paul reiterated his instruction that Titus teach this principle.

Prayer Focus: Lord, help me to always walk a walk that is equal to the talk I talk.   Amen.
Notes:

Spiritual Journal:

Week: Forty-one

Day: Wednesday

Book: Titus

Chapter: Three

Memory Verse: Seven

Principle: It is important to remember where we have come from and what we have been redeemed into so that we can live properly.

Outline:

> Verses 1-2 – Paul reminded us to be in proper respect of God-appointed authorities.
>
> Verses 3-8 – Our conversion is the basis for the requirements placed on our new lives.
>
> Verses 9-11 – Avoiding unfruitful and wrong ideas and conversation is a must.
>
> Verses 12-15 – Paul's personal notes as he closes this letter remind us that the issues addressed are real-life principles, not just ethereal ideas.

Prayer Focus: Lord, help me to always keep my life in proper focus as to what You have done in and for me.   Amen.

Notes:

Spiritual Journal:

Week: Forty-one
Day: Thursday
Book: Philemon
Chapter: One
Memory Verse: Six
Principle: In this personal letter, Paul asked Philemon to forgive Onesimus, apparently a run-away slave who had been converted under Paul's prison ministry. The principle is very simply that we must forgive as God has forgiven.
Outline:

> Verses 1-7 – Paul's greeting and thanksgiving are deliberately worded to encourage Philemon to respond generously to his request.
>
> Verses 8-16 – Paul framed his request in such a way as to let Philemon know that the apostle is not demanding nor even asking for anything beyond what should be expected.
>
> Verses 17-22 – Paul emphasized that the request was based not only on Philemon's Christian responsibility, but also on Paul's personal request and their friendship.
>
> Verses 23-25 – He concluded the letter with personal greetings from other friends of Philemon.

Prayer Focus: Lord, help me to always remember what a great sin debt You have blotted out of my account so I can be properly generous when forgiving others. Amen.
Notes:

Spiritual Journal:

Week: Forty-one
Day: Friday
Book: Hebrews
Chapter: One
Memory Verse: Three
Principle: Jesus is the apex of God's Kingdom and the ultimate communication to man
from God.
Outline:
Verses 1-3 – Jesus is the exact revelation of the Father and, therefore, the ultimate
communication from heaven to mankind.
Verses 4-14 – Jesus is superior to the angels in that:
a) The angels are not called sons;
b) The angels were made as ministers, not rulers;
c) The angels were not part of the creative process;
d) The angels are not invited to sit at the Father's hand; and
e) The angels are not promised to have their enemies subdued.
Prayer Focus: Lord, help me to always keep the exalted position of Jesus in mind; I need
to know that I serve a big God.   Amen.
Notes:

Spiritual Journal:

Week: Forty-two
Day: Monday
Book: Hebrews
Chapter: Two
Memory Verse: Seventeen
Principle: Even though Christ is highly exalted above the angels, He willingly took the nature of humanity so He could identify with mankind and redeem us.
Outline:

Verses 1-4 – The previous chapter made the point that Jesus is highly exalted above the angels; this chapter opens by stressing that if the Old Testament (which according to Hebrew legend was delivered by angels) was reverenced how much more must the New Testament (which came through Jesus and His church) be esteemed.

Verses 5-8 – The original dominion granted to man in creation illustrates the special place the human race has in the plan of God; however, man does not presently stand in his original position of authority.

Verses 9-13 – Jesus purposely left His position above the angels and took a lower position so that He could identify with mankind.

Verses 14-18 – Through the identification with mankind, Jesus was able to bring us redemption.

Prayer Focus: Lord, help me to see in Your incarnation the power of redemption to restore me to the original position of dominion from which the human race has fallen. Amen.

Notes:

Spiritual Journal:

Week: Forty-two
Day: Tuesday
Book: Hebrews
Chapter: Three
Memory Verse: Fourteen
Principle: Although the chapter does not draw its conclusion from the person of Moses, he is introduced as being another spiritual standard which is exceeded by Christ. The point of the chapter – that it is possible to begin in faith but fail to finish that way as illustrated by the Israelites, who didn't make it through the forty years of wanderings in the Sinai Desert – could have easily been drawn from Moses' life when he, too, failed to enter the Promised Land.

Outline:

Verses 1-6 – Moses and Jesus are compared using two different illustrations – a house to its builder and a servant to a son in the house. In both cases, it is obvious that Jesus is far superior to Moses, the great man of faith and heritage.

Verses 7-19 – The church is admonished to learn from the example of the Israelites who failed to enter the Promised Land, that they must hold to their faith to obtain the promises of God.

Prayer Focus: Lord, help me to keep my heart open and my faith out so that I will not fall short of obtaining the promises You have in store for me. Amen.

Notes:

Spiritual Journal:

Week: Forty-two
Day: Wednesday
Book: Hebrews
Chapter: Four
Memory Verse: Sixteen
Principle: The promises of God are not automatic; they can be forfeited through neglect and unbelief or they can be obtained by faith and bold appropriation.
Outline:
> Verses 1-2 – Believers are admonished to be cautious not to miss the promises as did the Israelites who lacked faith.
>
> Verses 3-5 – The point is stressed that God deliberately kept them from receiving the promises because of their unbelief.
>
> Verses 6-10 – The opportunity to enter into the promises of God is still a reality and a possibility; Joshua (mistranslated "Jesus" in some Bibles) did not complete the promise of God by taking the people into the Promised Land – many years after Joshua, there was still prophecy of promises awaiting God's people.
>
> Verses 11-13 – In light of the fact that God sees into the secrets of our hearts, believers are encouraged to diligently desire to fully obtain the promises of God.
>
> Verses 14-16 – Because Jesus does relate to our human state and needs, we are encouraged to bravely ask for His provision.

Prayer Focus: Lord, I ask for You to help me be bold enough to come to You and obtain the promises which You have for me and desire to give to me.   Amen.
Notes:

Spiritual Journal:

Week: Forty-two
Day: Thursday
Book: Hebrews
Chapter: Five
Memory Verse: Nine
Principle: If the human system of religion worked well, how much more will the divine intervention of God benefit those who are willing to give up their ignorance and receive the full knowledge of what God has done in Christ.
Outline:

> Verses 1-4 – The human priesthood through Aaron, although divinely appointed, was imperfect through the sinful nature of the ones appointed as representatives between God and man.
>
> Verses 5-6 – Christ was a priest after a different order – that of Melchisedec.
>
> Verses 7-10 – The incarnation into the human situation followed by exaltation to the divine realm perfected Christ as the effective high priest.
>
> Verses 11-14 – The believers lacked the spiritual depth and maturity to understand the principles and concepts being expressed in this epistle.

Prayer Focus: Lord, help me to go beyond milk and take a solid diet of Your instruction so I can know how to benefit fully from the Melchisedec priesthood of Christ. Amen.

Notes:

Spiritual Journal:

Week: Forty-two
Day: Friday
Book: Hebrews
Chapter: Six
Memory Verse: Twelve
Principle: Even though some will commit apostasy, there is a brighter hope for those who choose to believe and anchor into the security of God's promises.
Outline:

Verses 1-3 – Following the thought from the previous chapter, these verses encourage the believer to go beyond the "milk stage" and mature to the "meat stage" of the Christian life.

Verses 4-6 – Although these verses are often sources of concern for many, if they are properly understood, they should not be upsetting or reason for worry. The conditions for apostasy described here are so very stringent that it would actually be a rarity that anyone would qualify. Also note that the verse reads that it is impossible to renew them to repentance. This passage has often been misread to say that it is impossible for God to save them; however, it really says that it is impossible to get them to repent and ask for salvation. The problem is with the stubbornness of human will rather than a fault in divine grace.

Verses 7-9 – An illustration drawn from nature illustrates that the rain falls on the good herbs as well as on the thorny plants; the point is that there is a much better possibility that the reader will blossom as a good believer than as an apostate.

Verses 10-12 – With the encouragement of the preceding verses in mind and knowing the faithfulness of God to honor our efforts for Him, the believer is admonished to produce good works of faith and patience.

Verses 13-18 – Two unchangeable factors make God's promises unquestionable: His person and His Word.

Verses 19-20 – Based on a naval illustration of an anchor which firmly holds a ship in the area where it is moored, our faith anchors us to Christ, who has entered into the very presence of God in the Holy of Holies.

Prayer Focus: Lord, rather than falling into apostasy, I want to anchor into Your positive promises; help me to manifest the faith and patience to do so. Amen.

Notes and Spiritual Journal:

Week: Forty-three

Day: Monday

Book: Hebrews

Chapter: Seven

Memory Verse: Twenty-two

Principle: The priesthood of Jesus after the order of Melchisedec supersedes the Aaronic priesthood and establishes a superior relationship with God.

Outline:

Verses 1-4 – The uniqueness of the historical character Melchisedec is described in that:

a) He was the king of righteousness and the priest of peace.

b) He was a great enough figure for the patriarch Abraham to be willing to pay him tithes.

c) He is considered to have a perpetual priesthood since there is no record of his genealogy.

Verses 5-10 – The superiority of Melchisedec's priesthood over that of the Aaronic priesthood is demonstrated in that Levi symbolically tithed to Melchisedec when his ancestor Abraham gave offerings to him.

Verses 11-21 – When we realize that Jesus came as a priest but not from the descendants of Aaron, we understand that His priesthood was a prophetic fulfillment of the Melchisedec priesthood and that the ineffectual laws associated with the Aaronic priesthood are no longer in force.

Verses 22-28 – The weak, sinful, temporary priests have been replaced by Christ, who is perfect – without infirmity or fault.

Prayer Focus: Lord, help me to realize fully what it means to have Christ as my high priest, ever making intercession for me. Amen.

Notes:

Spiritual Journal:

Week: Forty-three
Day: Tuesday
Book: Hebrews
Chapter: Eight
Memory Verse: Ten
Principle: Not only has the priesthood been upgraded, the very covenant through which God deals with man has been rewritten.

Outline:

Verse 1 – The whole issue of Christ's priesthood boils down to the fact that He is a priest seated in heaven; this point denotes two important factors concerning His priesthood:

a) His being seated signifies that His priesthood is a finished work; there was no chair in the Old Testament Temple for the priest to sit on because his work was never complete.

b) The fact that He is in heaven while the other priests served in the earthly Temple demonstrates that His work is the reality which all the previous priesthood merely symbolized.

Verses 2-5 – The fact that the instructions for building the earthly Temple had to be meticulously followed in order to carefully reduplicate the pattern of the heavenly tabernacle showed that the earthly priesthood and system of sacrifices were only symbolic of God's real plan of salvation in heaven.

Verses 6-13 – A new covenant, in which the spirit of man is brought into the personal knowledge of God, was established in Christ.

Prayer Focus: Lord, help me to never try to live by the symbolic when the prophetic fulfillment and perfected covenant are mine to enjoy.   Amen.

Notes:

Spiritual Journal:

Week: Forty-three
Day: Wednesday
Book: Hebrews
Chapter: Nine
Memory Verse: Fourteen
Principle: Every element of Old Testament worship was symbolic of the coming plan of salvation in Christ; the important area of our focus is not to be on the Old Testament symbol but on the New Testament fulfillment.
Outline:

Verses 1-5 – Although all the elements in the Holy Place (the main chamber of the Temple) were symbolic, the author of Hebrews opts not to explain them because he wants to get to the issue of importance, the salvation plan demonstrated in the Holy of Holies (the inner chamber of the Temple).

Verses 6-12 – The high priest's annual entrance into the Holy of Holies with the sacrificial blood signified the entrance into the very presence of God and also the entrance into the inner recesses of the human spirit – gates which have now been unlocked by the sacrificial offering of Christ's blood.

Verses 13-22 – The death of Christ (embodied in His blood) established the last will and testament of His redemptive plan for man.

Verses 23-28 – Although Jesus fulfilled the symbolism of the Old Testament sacrifice system, His sacrificial death established a permanent salvation which replaced the temporal ritual cleansing of the former priesthood.

Prayer Focus: Lord, thank you for Your sacrificial plan for my redemption; help me to never fail to fully appropriate the benefits of this new covenant. Amen.
Notes:

Spiritual Journal:

Week: Forty-three

Day: Thursday

Book: Hebrews

Chapter: Ten

Memory Verse: Thirty-eight

Principle: Although Christ has done all that needs to be and can be done, He still leaves us with the responsibility to live the life of faith that appropriates His finished work; if we fail in this area, we fail in our Christian lives.

Outline:

Verses 1-18 – The once-for-all nature of Christ's sacrifice is again contrasted with the repetitive character of the Old Testament system which demanded repeated sacrifices that were unable to remove sin.

Verses 19-25 – An aggressive response on our part is in order, considering the free gift of salvation which God has provided for us.

Verses 26-31 – However, this free gift of salvation does not give us license to continue sinning; there is no other sacrifice available if we receive the gift and then disregard the cross.

Verses 32-37 – The church is reminded of the hardships they have already endured as believers and is encouraged to maintain their faith in the face of continued hardships.

Verses 38-39 – The determination to live by faith in Christ is a life-and-death decision.

Prayer Focus: Lord, help me to determine to live by faith and never to draw back into perdition or to willingly sin against Your precious blood-bought salvation. Amen.

Notes:

Spiritual Journal:

Week: Forty-three
Day: Friday
Book: Hebrews
Chapter: Eleven
Memory Verse: Six

Principle: Verse one of this chapter usually is considered "the" definition of faith; verse thirty-five of the previous chapter defines faith as the kind of confidence in God which has great reward; verse eleven of this chapter describes Sarah's faith as her trust in the faithfulness of God. In the rest of the discussion, faith is set forth as a simple matter of believing that God is going to do what He says that He will do.

Outline:

Verses 1-2 – Faith is introduced as not just an ethereal concept but something a lot more substantial than most of us perceive.

Verse 3 – Jesus taught us to have the God kind of faith; the author here suggests that believers can have the kind of faith which God used to create the universe.

Verses 4-31 – Various Old Testament personalities are used as illustrations of how faith can bring great results in the lives of believers. It is interesting to note that each of the individuals described as having faith was also a person of action, disproving the false concept that faith and works can be separated.

Verses 32-38 – Moving away from specific examples, the lesson on faith begins to focus on the relationship between faith and suffering. Three levels are distinguished:

a) Some were delivered *from* their suffering (The mouths of lions were stopped, etc.);

b) Some were delivered *in* their suffering (They maintained a testimony that the world was not worthy of their presence even though they continued to endure the suffering); and

c) Others were delivered *through* their suffering (They refused physical deliverance in order to obtain a better resurrection).

Verses 39-40 – The New Testament believers are encouraged that the faith promised to us even exceeds what has been demonstrated by any of the great faith heroes of the Old Testament.

Prayer Focus: Lord, even more than anything which I could obtain for myself through my faith, I want to please You, and I understand that that can only happen by faith; help me to have real faith. Amen.

Notes and Spiritual Journal:

Week: Forty-four
Day: Monday
Book: Hebrews
Chapter: Twelve
Memory Verse: One
Principle: Applied faith translates into lives of purpose, diligence, and purity.
Outline:

        Verses 1-2 – We are told to see the examples of faith set forth in the previous chapter but to focus our gaze on Jesus Himself because He is the foundation and goal of our faith.

        Verses 3-4 – One of the aspects gained when focusing on Jesus will be strength to endure opposition and difficulty.

        Verses 5-11 – It is important to maturely accept the correction which comes with chastening from the Lord.

        Verses 12-17 – Some of the pitfalls which can entrap a believer who becomes weary in his Christian faith due to failing to run with faith include:
        a) Bitterness against other believers
        b) Perversion of morals
        c) Lack of recognition of spiritual treasures

        Verses 18-24 – The heavenly nature of the covenant relationship with Christ is contrasted with the fearsome nature of the first covenant given on Mount Sinai.

        Verses 25-29 – Even though the Old Testament covenant has been replaced, it is imperative to remember that God has not personally changed; He is still the consuming fire seen on Mount Sinai and must be served with reverence and godly fear. The benefit of the new covenant is that He grants us grace through which to acceptably serve Him.

Prayer Focus: Lord, help me to keep my focus on You as the author and finisher of my faith so that I can properly live out my faith. Amen.

Notes:

Spiritual Journal:

Week: Forty-four
Day: Tuesday
Book: Hebrews
Chapter: Thirteen
Memory Verse: Eight
Principle: Practical day-to-day living demonstrates our faith life.
Outline:

       Verses 1-7 – Everyday relationships are great indicators of our faith:

           a) Hospitality to others

           b) Consideration for those in prison

           c) Marital relationships

           d) Respect for authority

       Verses 8-9 – Even though men's doctrines may change, there is a consistency of truth in Christ.

       Verses 10-14 – Jesus' sacrifice is again contrasted with the imperfect sacrificial system of the Old Testament.

       Verses 15-19 – Praise to God, submission to authority, and intercession for fellow believers constitute the New Testament obligations parallel to the Old Testament offering of sacrifices.

       Verses 20-21 – Perfection is the ultimate result of the faith relationship with Christ.

       Verses 22-25 – The letter closes with personal comments and a blessing.

Prayer Focus: Lord, help me to never try to separate or isolate my faith life from my daily living. Amen.
Notes:

Spiritual Journal:

Week: Forty-four
Day: Wednesday
Book: James
Chapter: One
Memory Verse: Twenty-two
Principle: In this letter which contains advice concerning the "where the rubber meets the road" application of the gospel principles, we are told how to turn the gospel we hear into the gospel we do.
Outline:
Verse 1 – When James introduced himself, he identified his ministry as being basically to the Jewish church; however, he does not exclude any believer – gentile or Jew – from his teachings.

Verses 2-4 – The ability to handle temptation is based on how convinced we are that all things are working out for our good.

Verses 5-8 – God is ready to give wisdom to those with unwavering faith in Him.

Verses 9-11 – Whether in a high or low position, all men must keep their human frailty in mind in order to avoid the pitfall of self-reliance.

Verses 12-16 – At its very root, temptation is actually self-induced and should be treated immediately – before it matures into sin and destruction.

Verses 17-18 – The good plan and purpose of God must be kept in focus in order to properly monitor our conduct and lifestyle.

Verses 19-21 – God's Word, not our words, must be what dominates our lives.

Verses 22-25 – Hearing the Word of God without applying it is like looking into a mirror but failing to correct what we see.

Verses 26-27 – Religion is action and lifestyle, not just theology.

Prayer Focus: Lord, help me to keep my actions in line with Your Word. Amen.
Notes:

Spiritual Journal:

Week: Forty-four
Day: Thursday
Book: James
Chapter: Two
Memory Verse: Twenty-six
Principle: Works without faith can be sinful and faith without works will be dead.
Outline:

       Verses 1-9 – Human ambition and respect for position result in sin.

       Verses 10-13 – Trying to keep the Law through human effort results in sin guilt.

       Verses 14-26 – Faith without corresponding action is useless. It is interesting that James cites as examples of works, the obedient actions of two people whom the book of Hebrews cites for demonstrating faith.

Prayer Focus: Lord, help me to have works that prove my faith but not simply works for works' sake. Amen.

Notes:

Spiritual Journal:

Week: Forty-four
Day: Friday
Book: James
Chapter: Three
Memory Verse: Thirteen
Principle: Our tongues are possibly the biggest indicators of who we really are; if they are controlled, our whole personality is under control.
Outline:
> Verses 1-8 – James begins his discussion on the tongue by describing the seeming impossibility of controlling the tongue while stressing the necessity of doing so.
>
> Verses 9-12 – The deceptive nature of the tongue which tries to bless and curse at the same time is exposed.
>
> Verses 13-18 – What we present as wisdom can be divine or demonic; the fruit of our so-called wisdom will verify its true source and nature.

Prayer Focus: Lord, take control of my tongue and bridle it so that my wisdom will unquestionably be from God. Amen.
Notes:

Spiritual Journal:

Week: Forty-five
Day: Monday
Book: James
Chapter: Four
Memory Verse: Ten
Principle: God resists the proud but gives grace to the humble; it is our inner heart
attitude which produces a relationship with the Lord which He will reward.
Outline:

Verses 1-6 – Sinfulness in our hearts and lives results in unanswered prayers.

Verses 7-10 – Having proactive faith – aggressively approaching God while
actively avoiding evil – results in our positive acceptance by God.

Verses 11-12 – Speaking evil of others is essentially speaking evil of the Law and
the Lawgiver.

Verses 13-16 – We must remember that God, not our plans, is sovereign.

Verse 17 – There is a sin of omission as well as a sin of commission.

Prayer Focus: Lord, I do want You to be close to me; help me to always remember that it
is my responsibility to stay close to You.   Don't let me forget the little saying, "If
God seems a long way off, who moved?"   Amen.
Notes:

Spiritual Journal:

Week: Forty-five
Day: Tuesday
Book: James
Chapter: Five
Memory Verse: Sixteen
Principle: It is possible to live in human bodies and yet achieve divine accomplishments.
Outline:

> Verses 1-6 – The wealthy who rely on their financial power will fail.
>
> Verses 7-11 – Patience – even to the point of longsuffering endurance – is the key to achieving through faith.
>
> Verses 12-16 – Practical responses based on our faith life are given for each situation which can confront a believer.
>
> Verses 17-18 – An Old Testament example is given to prove that a frail human can indeed succeed in the arena of faith.
>
> Verses 19-20 – It is the believer's responsibility to rescue the fallen brother.

Prayer Focus: Lord, help me to stop using my humanity as an excuse and to use my faith to accomplish the goals You have set for me.   Amen.
Notes:

Spiritual Journal:

Week: Forty-five
Day: Wednesday
Book: I Peter
Chapter: One
Memory Verse: Twenty-three
Principle: This whole chapter focuses around the fact that what God has prepared for us in our salvation is incorruptible – He has given us an incorruptible inheritance which was bought with an incorruptible price. This incorruptible quality is not to be interpreted to mean that it is impossible for us to spoil God's plan but should be understood to mean that His plan in and of itself is perfect.
Outline:
> Verses 1-4 – Peter's greeting and blessing introduces the theme that we have an incorruptible inheritance (one which cannot be defiled or spoiled) awaiting us.
>
> Verses 5-7 – God's good plan for our lives includes His provision for our preservation as we face trials and temptations.
>
> Verses 8-12 – Our experience of salvation and redemption is a privilege which the prophets of old greatly desired even though they did not get to experience it.
>
> Verses 13-17 – In light of the redemption we have received, we are called upon to be holy in thought, word, and action.
>
> Verses 18-20 – Our salvation was through the incorruptible blood of Christ.
>
> Verses 21-25 – Our new lives are a result of the incorruptible Word of God which dwells in us.

Prayer Focus: Lord, everything on Your part of my salvation has been incorruptible; help me not to corrupt it on my end. Amen.
Notes:

Spiritual Journal:

Week: Forty-five
Day: Thursday
Book: I Peter
Chapter: Two
Memory Verse: Nine
Principle: Peter uses several analogies (babies needing milk, stones of a building resting on a foundation stone, sheep being cared for by a shepherd) to illustrate the relationship of dependence we must have on Christ.
Outline:

> Verses 1-3 – The incorruptible Word of God is to a believer what milk is to a baby.

> Verses 4-8 – Using a tradition about a stone which was discarded during the building of Solomon's Temple, Peter illustrates the fact that Christ is the foundation of our faith even though He has been rejected and crucified.

> Verses 9-10 – We have been transformed from essentially having no meaning to having great significance in the Kingdom of God.

> Verses 11-20 – Practical application of our redeemed personality in our relationships with the outside world, with the family of God, and with our business dealings separates us from evildoers.

> Verses 21-25 – Christ is not only our example for how to live but also the source of our ability to live this new life.

Prayer Focus: Lord, help me to never try to stand alone but to always rely upon You, just as a building block rests upon the foundation.   Amen.
Notes:

Spiritual Journal:

Week: Forty-five
Day: Friday
Book: I Peter
Chapter: Three
Memory Verse: Twelve

Principle: There is a victory in the spiritual realm which supersedes whatever conflict may exist in the physical: women with the proper spiritual qualities can win their husbands without external tactics; husbands will find that their spiritual qualities are limited by their relationships toward their wives; and a good conscience guarantees victory even when the believer is persecuted while doing good.

Outline:

Verses 1-6 – Wives are to win their husbands through their inner spiritual qualities and beauty.

Verse 7 – Husbands are to guarantee their prayers by maintaining proper relations with their wives.

Verses 8-13 – Practicing proper, good actions and refraining from improper, bad actions toward others will be observed and rewarded or judged by the Lord.

Verses 14-17 – Even when we are persecuted for our good works, our pure conscience is a guarantee of victory.

Verses 18-22 – Christ is an example of one who suffered for righteousness and won victory not only for Himself but also for all the souls who were held in captivity.

Prayer Focus: Lord, help me to have the inner quality which will win outer victories. Amen.

Notes:

Spiritual Journal:

Week: Forty-six
Day: Monday
Book: I Peter
Chapter: Four
Memory Verse: Eight
Principle: Christ's self-giving love is the pinnacle of the Christian life; it covers all our
individual sins and all the sins committed against us.
Outline:
Verses 1-6 – Christ's sacrificial love for us makes it possible for us to live lives
separated from the sins we once committed.
Verses 7-9 – In light of the prophetic time we live in, we are commanded to
concentrate on the quality and quantity of our love life.
Verses 10-11 – We are directed to fully use everything which we have been given
by God; we cannot be stingy with the gifts we have received.
Verses 12-16 – We are directed to carefully guard ourselves, that there be no
reason for us to suffer for wrongdoing; if we are to suffer, it must be
because of our good deeds.
Verses 17-19 – Judgment and evaluation of our lives must come within the
context of the church, not in the outside world; if the church cannot pass
the test, the unsaved will certainly be without a chance.
Prayer Focus: Lord, I realize that You are now my redeemer but will someday be my
judge; help me to live a life now which will stand through Your judgment then.
Amen.
Notes:

Spiritual Journal:

Week: Forty-six

Day: Tuesday

Book: I Peter

Chapter: Five

Memory Verse: Ten

Principle: Proper relationships and attitudes within the Body of Christ will result in our being established by the Lord.

Outline:

> Verses 1-4 – Pastors are commanded to care for church members willingly and with love, without ulterior motives.
>
> Verses 5-9 – Proper attitudes of humility, dependence upon God, and resistance of the devil are required of church members.
>
> Verses 10-11 – The end result is that Christ Himself will establish us in the Kingdom of God.
>
> Verses 12-14 – Personal greetings and blessings conclude the letter.

Prayer Focus: Lord, I want to be established in Your Kingdom; help me to properly fill my place here so that I will have a place there.   Amen.

Notes:

Spiritual Journal:

Week: Forty-six
Day: Wednesday
Book: II Peter
Chapter: One
Memory Verse: Four

Principle: We have a divine call through the unquestionable Word of God and a promise that the power of God will work in us to take us through the various stages of spiritual maturity.

Outline:

Verses 1-2 – Peter opens the letter with a greeting and a blessing.

Verses 3-4 – Peter contrasted the great promises and provisions which we possess with the corruption from which we have been delivered. We have two possible destinies: the very nature of God or corruption. When describing the two avenues which lead toward those two destinations (the knowledge of God and lust), Peter uses the same prefix on the two Greek words, rendering the thought that we will either have an all-encompassing knowledge of God or we will have an all-encompassing lust for natural things.

Verses 5-11 – Maturity in the Christian life takes a diligent effort on the believer's part to add new qualities at each level of development he has reached.

Verses 12-15 – The importance of this message to Peter is demonstrated in the fact that he emphasized this teaching when he realized that he only had a short time remaining in his physical life.

Verses 16-21 – He spoke of having unquestionable confidence in the prophetic Word of God after he heard the audible voice of God at Jesus' transfiguration.

Prayer Focus: Lord, corruption is certainly not how I want my life to be characterized; help me to follow after Your knowledge so that the divine nature can be revealed in me. Amen.

Notes:

Spiritual Journal:

Week: Forty-six
Day: Thursday
Book: II Peter
Chapter: Two
Memory Verse: Nine
Principle: Just as surely as there is great reward for faith and righteousness, there is certain destruction for unrighteousness and heresy.
Outline:

> Verses 1-3 – Peter made it clear that future false prophets and false teachers would lead many away from the truth.
>
> Verses 4-9 – Old Testament examples were cited to prove that God is able to deliver the righteous while executing judgment on the wicked.
>
> Verses 10-14 – The detailed description of the false prophets and teachers paints a picture of the corrupt nature Peter attributed to them in the previous chapter.
>
> Verses 15-19 – Not only are the false prophets and teachers corrupt in themselves, they have a corrupting influence upon all who heed their words.
>
> Verses 20-22 – The desperately hopeless situation of those who turn away from the knowledge of God is graphically portrayed.

Prayer Focus: Lord, help me to carefully avoid following those who will lead me into corruption and help me never to lead anyone else wrongly. Amen.
Notes:

Spiritual Journal:

Week: Forty-six
Day: Friday
Book: II Peter
Chapter: Three
Memory Verse: Nine
Principle: When we see the big picture and realize that our temporal lives are such a minute part of God's eternal plan and that He will soon dissolve and remake the entire physical creation, we must resolve to live our lives with a totally new perspective.
Outline:
> Verses 1-2 – Having warned his readers about the deception of the false prophets and teachers, Peter reminds them to give heed to the teachings of the holy prophets and apostles.
>
> Verses 3-7 – He reminded the church that there would be those who would challenge prophetic teaching, claiming that it would never be fulfilled.
>
> Verses 8-10 – Even though He seems to delay, God will fulfill His Word; and when He does, it will happen suddenly, giving no time for the critics to reconsider.
>
> Verses 11-18 – With eternity in perspective, we are challenged to live lives of purity, increasing in the knowledge of God (the remedy for corruption which he presented in the first chapter of this epistle).

Prayer Focus: Lord, it is so easy to lose the eternal perspective and to think that the temporal things around us are all that count; help me to get everything into perspective with the big picture.   Amen.
Notes:

Spiritual Journal:

Week: Forty-seven

Day: Monday

Book: I John

Chapter: One

Memory Verse: Seven

Principle: Just as turning on a light dispels darkness from a room, abiding in Christ eradicates sinfulness from our lives.

Outline:

Verses 1-4 – John establishes the validity of his message by showing that he personally knew Jesus during His earthly ministry.

Verses 5-10 – The issue of sinfulness which John deals with here must be understood in light of the Greek tense he employs. John is saying that a Christian who lives in the light of God does not live a life of habitual sinning; however, if he sins on particular occasions, he can confess those acts of sin and be forgiven and cleansed from them. A believer must never deny sin; if he does, he has negated his opportunity to be free from it.

Prayer Focus: Lord, I confess my sinful nature and my sinful acts – but more importantly, I confess and rely upon the righteous nature that You have imparted to me. Amen.

Notes:

Spiritual Journal:

Week: Forty-seven
Day: Tuesday
Book: I John
Chapter: Two
Memory Verse: Seventeen

Principle: As John addresses the various members of the Body of Christ who are at different levels of maturity, it is interesting that he writes the same thing to both the most advanced (the fathers) and the new beginners (the little children or babies) – that they know Him. Everything else fades away in light of the importance of knowing Christ.

Outline:

Verses 1-2 – Because Christ dealt with our sins, believers can have confidence in their relationship with God.

Verses 3-6 – Our actions must line up with our confessions.

Verses 7-11 – The commandment of love is new in that it replaces the old listing of ordinances, but it is not new in that it has always been the summation and motivation of those regulations.

Verses 12-14 – The various segments of the congregation are addressed with admonitions concerning their relationships with Christ.

Verses 15-17 – Our attachments to the physical world must be judged in light of the fact that they are soon to pass away and that the only eternal element unto which we can attach ourselves is Christ.

Verses 18-29 – John warned the church concerning the liars which would deny Christ and draw them away from Him; at the same time, he encouraged them to rely upon the anointing of the Holy Spirit which dwells in them to reveal the truth to them. One indicator of who is from God and who is not is whether he is living a righteous life.

Prayer Focus: Lord, I want to mature, but I never want to move away from my child-like faith in and relationship with You. Amen.

Notes:

Spiritual Journal:

Week: Forty-seven
Day: Wednesday
Book: I John
Chapter: Three
Memory Verse: Two
Principle: It has been said that the only Bible verses we believe are the ones we act upon; this section of scripture seems to emphasize that point by saying that, unless we live righteous lives, we do not really believe in Christ.

Outline:

Verses 1-6 – If we really have the hope of the gospel within us, we will purify our lives; if we are abiding in Him, He will deal with our sinfulness.

Verses 7-10 – Do not be deceived into believing that a person who has Christ abiding in him can continue to live in sin.

Verses 11-18 – The love of God within the believer motivates him to act on behalf of a brother in need.

Verses 19-24 – A clean conscience, answered prayers, keeping the commandment of love, and the witness of the Holy Spirit are indicators of our good standing with the Lord.

Prayer Focus: Lord, help me to truly believe in You and to live my life in a way that unquestionably proves that I do. Amen.

Notes:

Spiritual Journal:

Week: Forty-seven
Day: Thursday
Book: I John
Chapter: Four
Memory Verse: Four
Principle: It may seem that this chapter has two focal points – the warning to avoid false spirits and heeding the testimony of the Holy Spirit, and the directive toward brotherly love. However, it really has only one: John was warning the reader to beware of any spirit which tried to convince the believer that his faith could be separated from his demonstration of Christian love.

Outline:

> Verses 1-3 – A warning against believing every spirit is given.
>
> Verses 4-6 – Our relationship with God, our ability to overcome the world, and our answers to prayer are indicators as to whether we are receiving a spirit of truth or a spirit of error.
>
> Verses 7-11 – The love of God toward us demands that we also love our brothers.
>
> Verses 12-17 – The love of God manifested in our lives is the proof that we have seen and know God.
>
> Verse 18 – Perfected love eliminates fearfulness about our salvation.
>
> Verses 19-21 – Lack of love proves that God is not in our lives.

Prayer Focus: Lord, help me not to be deceived by the spirit of the antichrist that would tell me that my theology or good deeds rather than my living in love is what proves my faith. Amen.

Notes:

Spiritual Journal:

Week: Forty-seven

Day: Friday

Book: I John

Chapter: Five

Memory Verse: Four

Principle: After his warnings about deceiving spirits and error, John concludes the book with a tremendous note of confidence; he repeatedly speaks of the victorious facts which we know and of the confidence we can have in Christ.

Outline:

Verses 1-5 – Our faith, or belief that Jesus is the Christ, is the key

a) To being born of God

b) Overcoming the world

c) Having true brotherly love

d) Being able to keep God's commandments

Verses 6-13 – In addition to the witness we have in heaven and the witness we have on earth, the believer has a witness within himself that he has eternal life. Also, John has given an additional testimony in writing this letter.

Verses 14-15 – We have confidence that we can pray and receive answers.

Verses 16-17 – Although he does not define the terms, John leaves his readers with instructions to pray for Christian brothers who have committed sins which are not considered sins unto death.

Verses 18-21 – He closed the letter with a tremendous word of victory and encouragement to believers:

a) That we do not have to be influenced by the enemy

b) That we can know the truth

c) That we can be certain that we have eternal life

Prayer Focus: Lord, help me to never slip away from the confidence and victory You have provided for me. Amen.

Notes:

Spiritual Journal:

Week: Forty-eight
Day: Monday
Book: II John
Chapter: One
Memory Verse: Six
Principle: Truth and love are the essential elements of the Christian faith.
Outline:

> Verses 1-3 – The greeting mentions love twice and truth four times, signifying the ultimate importance of these two qualities.
>
> Verses 4-6 – Fulfilling the commandments of Christ is summed up in walking in truth and living in love.
>
> Verses 7-11 – John warned his readers about the deceivers who deny that Christ has come in the flesh.
>
> Verses 12-13 – He closed the letter with a greeting and an expression of his desire to visit in person.

Prayer Focus: Lord, help me to always keep the faith and follow in truth and love. Amen.

Notes:

Spiritual Journal:

Week: Forty-eight

Day: Tuesday

Book: III John

Chapter: One

Memory Verse: Two

Principle: God's blessings are not automatic; they depend upon the kind of lives we are living.

Outline:

Verse 1 – The greeting carries over the theme of truth and love from the previous book.

Verse 2 – John prays a blessing on every area of Gaius' life: his finances, his physical health, and his spiritual and emotional wellbeing.

Verses 3-8 – A testimony is given to Gaius' faithfulness to God and his generosity to the Body of Christ. It is interesting to study all the other references to Gaius in the New Testament and see that they unanimously confirm his generous nature.

Verses 9-11 – John's comments concerning Diotrephes paint a completely different picture – one of a person whose life displays none of the qualities found in Gaius and who does not receive the blessings extended to Gaius.

Verse 12 – Demetrius is recognized as another individual of good character and report.

Verses 13-14 – John closed the letter with a blessing and an expression of his desire to visit in person.

Prayer Focus: Lord, help me to be like Gaius and Demetrius so that I can be in line for the kinds of blessings they received. Help me not to follow after the pattern of Diotrephes and lose all opportunity to be blessed. Amen.

Notes:

Spiritual Journal:

Week: Forty-eight

Day: Wednesday

Book: Jude

Chapter: One

Memory Verse: Twenty-one

Principle: Even in the face of great apostasy, through the power of the Holy Spirit, it is possible to not only keep the faith but to also spread it.

Outline:

> Verses 1-2 – Jude opens the letter with an identification of himself, a greeting, and a blessing.
>
> Verses 3-4 – In light of the apostasy which will become prevalent, he admonishes the believers to contend for the faith.
>
> Verses 5-7 – Several Old Testament examples are given to illustrate the point that individuals in good standing with God can fall from that place of favor and become objects of His judgment.
>
> Verses 8-16 – Jude graphically describes the polluted and polluting nature of the apostates and confirmed prophetically that they will be judged.
>
> Verses 17-23 – He encourages the believers to strengthen themselves through prayer in the Spirit and focusing their attention on Christ so that they can protect their own spiritual lives and make a difference in the lives of others.
>
> Verses 24-25 – The letter closes with a doxology which emphasizes God's ability to preserve the believer.

Prayer Focus: Lord, help me stand firm even when those around me fall and become corrupted; moreover, help me to be strong enough to help rescue others from falling. Amen.

Notes:

Spiritual Journal:

Week: Forty-eight
Day: Thursday
Book: Revelation
Chapter: One
Memory Verse: Three
Principle: Although it does contain futuristic prophecy, this book is not, as many suppose, a revelation of the future; it is a revelation of the highly exalted Christ and the fact that He is the key to understanding the past and the present as well as the future.
Outline:
> Verses 1-3 – The introduction confirms that the testimony of Christ to be shared in this book is from God and that it carries a blessing for all who read it, hear it read, and live by the revelation it contains.
>
> Verses 4-8 – John addresses the seven churches who are to receive the book and gives them a preview of the exalted position believers are to occupy in Christ.
>
> Verses 9-18 – John tells the story of his encounter with the risen Christ and describes the overwhelming glory of His exalted person.
>
> Verses 19-20 – The risen Christ directs John to write to the seven churches to tell them about the things which have been, things which are, and things which are to come.

Prayer Focus: Lord, help me to always see You in the middle and in charge of all that happens. Amen.
Notes:

Spiritual Journal:

Week: Forty-eight
Day: Friday
Book: Revelation
Chapter: Two
Memory Verse: Twenty-nine
Principle: God, who knows all our works and all our attitudes, speaks to us addressing each issue; we must hear and respond as the Spirit uncovers areas of concern.
Outline:
>
> Verses 1-7 – Even though the Ephesian church had a record of exposing and expelling those with false doctrine, God was not totally pleased with them because they had let go of their initial love for Him.
>
> Verses 8-11 – Jesus promised the church at Smyrna that, even though they were enduring persecution, it would only be for a limited time and that they would be rewarded with a crown of life.
>
> Verses 12-17 – The church at Pergamos was addressed because it allowed false teachers to remain active within their congregation.
>
> Verses 18-29 – The message to the church at Thyatira was two-fold: those who practice unrighteousness will be judged according to their wickedness (the harlot will be cast into the bed where she committed fornication, yet, this time, it will be a bed of sickness); the righteous must hold fast to their faith and will be rewarded for their overcoming faith.

Prayer Focus: Lord, help me to always be sensitive to hear Your Spirit as He speaks to me. Amen.

Notes:

Spiritual Journal:

Week: Forty-nine
Day: Monday
Book: Revelation
Chapter: Three
Memory Verse: Twenty-one
Principle: The coming of the Lord – whether He comes unexpectedly as a thief in the night or politely as a guest knocking at the door – is the pivotal factor that must be kept in consideration in all that we do and the way we live our lives.
Outline:

Verses 1-6 – The letter to the Sardis church is an encouragement to hold on to their faith and the promise of reward at the Lord's coming.

Verses 7-13 – The Philadelphia church is given the promise that an unclosable door of ministry is to be opened before them.

Verses 14-22 – The address to the Laodicean church warns them about their self-deception, which has given them a false self-confidence; they are admonished to invite Christ into their lives so that He can invite them into His victory.

Prayer Focus: Lord, help me to live every moment as if it were the one in which You are to return – because it may really be so!   Amen.
Notes:

Spiritual Journal:

Week: Forty-nine
Day: Tuesday
Book: Revelation
Chapter: Four
Memory Verse: Eleven
Principle: All of heaven's attention and focus is centered on the worship of God the
        Creator; we on earth should take a lesson from them.
Outline:
        Verse 1 – John is invited into the heavenly throne room of God.
        Verses 2-8 – God, His throne, the seven-fold Spirit of God, the sea of glass, and
            the four beasts (or living creatures) are described.
        Verses 9-11 – The worship given to the Father is described.
Prayer Focus: Lord, in heaven, You are continually receiving the highest form of praise;
        help me to adequately praise You on earth as well. Amen.
Notes:

Spiritual Journal:

Week: Forty-nine
Day: Wednesday
Book: Revelation
Chapter: Five
Memory Verse: Thirteen
Principle: In the previous chapter, the Father was worshipped because He is the Creator; in this chapter, Jesus is worshipped because He is the Redeemer.
Outline:

> Verses 1-4 – John was distressed because no one was worthy to open the book of revelation which the Father held in His hand.
>
> Verses 5-10 – One of the elders announced that, because of His redeeming sacrifice, Jesus was worthy to open the book. When He took the book, the elders and the living creatures began to worship Him for His redemptive act.
>
> Verses 11-14 – A universal chorus from heaven, earth, the underworld, and the sea joined the heavenly hosts in worshipping the Redeemer.

Prayer Focus: Lord, Your re-creative work in me is as wondrous as Your creative work in me; help me to never cease to praise You for it. Amen.
Notes:

Spiritual Journal:

Week: Forty-nine
Day: Thursday
Book: Revelation
Chapter: Six
Memory Verse: Seventeen

Principle: It has been said that history is "His story"; truly, the events of human history make no sense unless seen in the light of God's redemptive plan. As the seals on this book are opened, we see symbolically that the meaning of the events of history will remain a mystery without Christ as the key to history.

Outline:

Verses 1-2 – The first seal reveals a conqueror on a white horse who holds a bow but no arrows; this character symbolizes a false Christ who mimics the victorious Lord but who proves to be powerless in the final analysis.

Verses 3-4 – War is symbolized in the opening of the second seal.

Verses 5-6 – Famine appeared at the opening of the third seal.

Verses 7-8 – Death followed by Hell was revealed as the fourth seal was opened.

Verses 9-11 – The fifth seal spoke of the martyrs who had given their lives for the gospel and proclaimed that God's judgment would be delayed until their number was fulfilled.

Verses 12-17 – The opening of the sixth seal ushered in human dread of the pending divine judgment.

Prayer Focus: Lord, much of what I see going on around the world makes no sense; help me to see Your hand in the events of human history – past, present, and future. Amen.

Notes:

Spiritual Journal:

Week: Forty-nine
Day: Friday
Book: Revelation
Chapter: Seven
Memory Verse: Seventeen
Principle: This interlude between the opening of the sixth and the seventh seals demonstrates that God is active in His redemptive work at every point in human history and that His plan results in a choir of those redeemed from every nation, kindred, people, and tongue.
Outline:
> Verses 1-3 – Destruction was held back until God had sealed the ones He had marked for preservation.
>
> Verses 4-8 – Twelve thousand from each tribe of Israel were marked for divine protection and preservation. While the tribe of Dan is missing from this list, the original tribe of Joseph is represented twice through Manasses and Joseph.
>
> Verses 9-12 – A universal choir sang the praises of God.
>
> Verses 13-17 – God's personal loving care for those who have suffered for Him is described.

Prayer Focus: Lord, help me to remember that You have made a way of escape in every temptation and that You never allow anything greater than we can bear to come upon us; also help me to focus on the reward You have for me at the end of the race and not to be overcome by the pressure of the moment. Amen.
Notes:

Spiritual Journal:

Week: Fifty
Day: Monday
Book: Revelation
Chapter: Eight
Memory Verse: Four
Principle: Just as Joshua's attack on the city of Jericho consisted of six days with one march around the city and a seventh day with seven marches around the city, the pattern in Revelation is six seals with one event each, followed by a seventh seal with seven events; this pattern also occurs with the blowing of six trumpets followed by a seventh trumpet which consists of seven vials of judgment.
Outline:
> Verses 1-6 – God again delayed the judgment pending the prayers and intercession of the saints.
>
> Verse 7 – The first judgment was against the vegetation.
>
> Verses 8-9 – The second judgment was against the oceans and sea life.
>
> Verses 10-11 – The third judgment, Wormwood, was against the fresh-water sources.
>
> Verse 12 – The fourth judgment was against the heavenly bodies.
>
> Verse 13 – An angel announced woes concerning the three remaining judgments.

Prayer Focus: Lord, help me to realize that, even if they do not stop the inevitable, my prayers do make a difference. Amen.
Notes:

Spiritual Journal:

Week: Fifty
Day: Tuesday
Book: Revelation
Chapter: Nine
Memory Verse: Twenty
Principle: Just as Pharaoh's refusal to yield to Moses' demand to release the Israelites prolonged the plagues against Egypt, man's refusal to repent forces God to judge the earth.
Outline:

> Verses 1-12 – The fifth angel's trumpet released the hoards of demonic locusts which plagued mankind for five months. The king over this diabolic invasion is known by Greek and Hebrew names which mean "The Destroyer."

> Verses 13-19 – At the blast of the sixth angel's trumpet, an army of two hundred million horsemen was released to kill one third of the human race with fire, smoke, and brimstone from their mouths and to inflict injury upon the rest of the population with their serpent-like tails.

> Verses 20-21 – In spite of the extensive judgment, the human race refused to repent before the Lord.

Prayer Focus: Lord, make me quick to repent – not simply to avoid judgment, but in order to keep a right relationship with You. Amen.
Notes:

Spiritual Journal:

Week: Fifty
Day: Wednesday
Book: Revelation
Chapter: Ten
Memory Verse: Eleven
Principle: Jesus taught us that we would not understand some prophetic things until they actually began to take place; the sealing of the little book followed by the commandment to ingest the book and make a fresh prophecy reiterate this concept.
Outline:
> Verses 1-4 – John was forbidden to write down the words of the seven thunders which he heard when the radiant angel appeared with the little book.
>
> Verses 5-7 – The angel proclaimed that there was a mystery to God's plan which would remain unrevealed until it came to fulfillment.
>
> Verses 8-10 – Following the instructions of a heavenly voice, John took the book and ate it; although it was sweet in his mouth, it produced bitterness in his belly.
>
> Verse 11 – John was instructed that the prophetic ministry is to continue. Although not stated, the implication seems to be that it will continue until the ultimate fulfillment of all prophecy has come.

Prayer Focus: Lord, help me to always bear in mind that I don't have all the answers yet, so I shouldn't be too convinced that I have it all figured out; some prophecies will only be understood as they are played out in history.   Amen.
Notes:

Spiritual Journal:

Week: Fifty
Day: Thursday
Book: Revelation
Chapter: Eleven
Memory Verse: Seventeen
Principle: The majesty of God is revealed in both His redemptive plan and His righteous judgment of the wicked.
Outline:

Verses 1-2 – John was told to measure the Temple but to omit the outer court, signifying that this prophetic message dealing with a three-and-a-half-year period was related to the Jewish people rather than the gentiles.

Verses 3-12 – Two witnesses will proclaim the truth of God during this prophetic three-and-a-half-year period. Although they will demonstrate supernatural powers, the destroyer will wage war against them and kill them. During the three and a half days that their bodies remain unburied, the rulers of the nations will rejoice over their death; however, their resurrection and ascension to heaven will cause great fear among the nations.

Verses 13-14 – The blast of the second woe (sixth trumpet) will be an earthquake which destroys a tenth of the city of Jerusalem and results in seven thousand deaths.

Verses 15-19 – The blowing of the seventh trumpet evoked a tremendous response in heaven:

a) The twenty-four elders fell on their faces and worshipped God, proclaiming His majesty in both redemption and judgment.

b) The Temple was open and the Ark of the Covenant revealed.

c) Lightning, voices, thunder, an earthquake, and great hail occurred.

Prayer Focus: Lord, help me to always see Your majesty in all You do – whether it be in redemption or in judgment. Amen.
Notes:

Spiritual Journal:

Week: Fifty
Day: Friday
Book: Revelation
Chapter: Twelve
Memory Verse: Eleven
Principle: Man must always remember that, although he is the object of a cosmic battle between God and Satan, he has been given the resources for victory over the enemy.
Outline:

Verses 1-2 – A vision representing the nation of Israel and the birth of Christ is described.

Verses 3-4 – The fall of Satan and his demonic hosts is portrayed in a complementary vision.

Verses 5-9 – The two visions mesh into one which reveals the cosmic battle in which Christ ascended to heaven, Israel was shielded in the wilderness for a three-and-a-half-year period, and Satan and his angels were cast out of their position of authority in the heavenly places.

Verses 10-12 – In what almost seems to be a contradiction, salvation, strength, and the Kingdom of God are proclaimed and the believers are told to rejoice, as Satan has come to earth with great wrath; the point is that even in the midst of great onslaught, believers have the power to overcome.

Verses 13-17 – Satan attacked the nation of Israel, but, for three and a half years, she was divinely protected, and the earth itself defended her. Satan's resulting great anger led him to wage war against all believers.

Prayer Focus: Lord, help me to have so much confidence in You and Your provision for my deliverance that I can rejoice when I see that Satan has staged an attack against me. Amen.
Notes:

Spiritual Journal:

Week: Fifty-one
Day: Monday
Book: Revelation
Chapter: Thirteen
Memory Verse: Eight

Principle: In this chapter, John uses a lot of Old Testament symbolism (especially from the book of Daniel) to identify two beasts which will appear in the last days of human history. Identifying them and unraveling the mysteries of the symbolism are not the points of interest in the lesson today; rather, the objective is to see the universal influence which these evil powers will have and to note that the only possibility of resisting such a wicked force is to be listed in the Lamb's Book of Life.

Outline:

Verses 1-10 – John observed a beast rising from the sea, possibly suggesting that it is a power originating from the west (Mediterranean side) of Israel. This beast, based on the symbolism used, seems to be a political power representing the revival of the ancient world empires. It should be noted that all authority exercised by the beast is said to have been given to it, signifying that, even though it is a universal power, it is still not independent of God's authority. It is also important to note that its authority is limited to only three and a half years.

Verses 11-17 – A second beast appeared from the earth, possibly suggesting that it comes from either Israel itself or from Asia to the east (the land side). From the language used, it seems that this beast functions in the arena of religion rather than politics, unlike the first beast. Using his supernatural powers to garner loyalty for the first beast, he brings the entire population to a place of total dependence upon the beast to the point that no commerce can be transacted without the identification number issued by the beast.

Verse 18 – Although the scripture says that anyone with wisdom should understand the number of the beast, Bible students throughout history have never been able to come to a clear decision as to its meaning. It seems best to understand it as an attempt on man's part (symbolized by the number six) to take the place of God (symbolized by the triple use of the number, suggesting the Trinity).

Prayer Focus: Lord, as evil influences exert themselves, help me to remember that my name is in Your book and that You are ultimately in control. Amen.

Notes and Spiritual Journal:

Week: Fifty-one
Day: Tuesday
Book: Revelation
Chapter: Fourteen
Memory Verse: Seven
Principle: This chapter consists of the appearance of the Lamb, accompanied by the 144,000 witnesses, followed by the appearance of five angels. The sequence of these appearances seems to be a verification of God's pattern that Christ will always appear when it seems that evil has reached its zenith and that an opportunity for repentance is always extended before judgment begins.

Outline:
Verses 1-5 – The Lamb appeared with His 144,000 virtuous followers. They may be considered as "trophies" to witness to the fact that God is able to preserve a holy remnant even through the seemingly universal rule of evil.

Verses 6-7 – The first angel appeared to proclaim the gospel throughout the earth.

Verse 8 – The second angel appeared to proclaim the collapse of Babylon, the seat of the evil authority.

Verses 9-11 – The third angel proclaimed the doom of all who have yielded themselves to evil.

Verses 12-13 – A promise of peace is extended to those who have suffered for their faith.

Verses 14-16 – The fourth angel announced to the Son of Man that it was time to begin His harvest of the earth (symbolizing the rapture of the saints).

Verses 17-20 – The fifth angel collected the harvest of grapes (symbolizing the judgment of the unrighteous).

Prayer Focus: Lord, help me to always rely on Your power to help me remain pure even in the worst of circumstances. Amen.

Notes:

Spiritual Journal:

Week: Fifty-one
Day: Wednesday
Book: Revelation
Chapter: Fifteen
Memory Verse: Four

Principle: Judgment can never be independent of redemption – even as the last seven vials of God's wrath are being prepared for the final judgment of the earth, heaven's residents are singing the song of redemption and proclaiming that all nations shall come and worship God.

Outline:

Verse 1 – The seven angels who are to implement the last judgments are introduced.

Verses 2-4 – The victorious believers sing the song of Moses and the song of the Lamb.

Verses 5-8 – The heavenly Temple is opened and filled with the glory of God as the seven angels ready themselves to inflict the final judgments on the earth.

Prayer Focus: Lord, help me to always see both Your redemption in light of Your judgment and Your judgment in light of Your redemption. Amen.

Notes:

Spiritual Journal:

Week: Fifty-one
Day: Thursday
Book: Revelation
Chapter: Sixteen
Memory Verse: Five
Principle: Judgment is a manifestation of the righteousness of God.
Outline:

> Verse 1 – A voice from the Temple (presumably God's) commands the angels to release the judgments.
>
> Verse 2 – The first angel released sores upon men.
>
> Verse 3 – The second angel released judgment upon the seas and all ocean life was destroyed.
>
> Verses 4-7 – When the third angel released judgment upon the fresh water, the righteousness of God's judgment was proclaimed.
>
> Verses 8-9 – The fourth angel released judgment upon the sun so that men were scorched with intense heat.
>
> Verses 10-11 – When the fifth angel released judgment upon the seat of the beast's kingdom, men blasphemed God.
>
> Verses 12-16 – When the sixth angel poured out his vial upon the Euphrates River, it dried up to make a path for the attack by the kings of the East and for the release of the three frog spirits which will draw the nations of the world to the Battle of Armageddon.
>
> Verses 17-21 – The seventh angel poured out his vial into the air, resulting in the fall of Babylon, the disappearance of the islands, the collapse of the mountains, and a deluge of great hail stones.

Prayer Focus: Lord, Hebrews teaches us that our earthly fathers correct us according to their own pleasure but that Your correction is righteous; help me to always recognize Your righteousness, even when You have to correct me.   Amen.

Notes:

Spiritual Journal:

Week: Fifty-one
Day: Friday
Book: Revelation
Chapter: Seventeen
Memory Verse: Fourteen
Principle: Even though evil may establish a great front, it will always fall before the forces of God; sometimes God even uses the forces of evil to destroy themselves in fulfillment of His plan.
Outline:

Verses 1-6 – The blasphemous nature of the Great Harlot is portrayed.

Verses 7-15 – The identity of the Great Harlot is revealed through Old Testament symbolism, which seems to indicate that she represents a power (possibly religious) which has universal support and seemingly total control of the ten kings. Although actual identification of the Great Harlot may be unclear, the important point is that she is a force which adamantly wars against the Lamb.

Verses 16-17 – God turns the hearts of the kings so that they will fight against the Great Harlot.

Verse 18 – She is identified with the city of great influence, which is identified as Babylon in the next chapter.

Prayer Focus: Lord, thank you for this insight into the truth that evil will ultimately implode upon itself. Amen.

Notes:

Spiritual Journal:

Week: Fifty-two
Day: Monday
Book: Revelation
Chapter: Eighteen
Memory Verse: Five
Principle: There is an old saying that the wheels of God may turn slowly but they grind very fine.   Even though it may seem that sin is going unnoticed, God remembers each offense and will judge all of them.
Outline:
        Verses 1-3 – An angel proclaimed the judgment of Babylon.
        Verses 4-8 – A voice from heaven (possibly God's) announced the city's immediate doom.
        Verses 9-10 – The kings of the earth bewailed her destruction.
        Verses 11-19 – The merchants of the earth lamented her demise.
        Verse 20 – The inhabitants of heaven, on the other hand, were directed to rejoice over the fall of the evil city.
        Verses 21-24 – A mighty angel symbolically showed Babylon's end by casting a millstone into the sea and proclaimed that judgment was due because of the sorceries which had deceived the nations and resulted in the shedding of the martyrs' blood.
Prayer Focus: Lord, help me to carefully heed Your warning to come out from among the iniquities of this present life.   Amen.
Notes:

Spiritual Journal:

Week: Fifty-two
Day: Tuesday
Book: Revelation
Chapter: Nineteen
Memory Verse: Sixteen
Principle: Our God is omnipotent, and He reigns!
Outline:

> Verses 1-6 – All heaven rejoiced at the righteousness of God which was demonstrated in the judgment of the Great Harlot.
>
> Verses 7-9 – Joy was expressed over the announcement of the marriage of the Lamb.
>
> Verse 10 – John was corrected for misplacing the focus of his worship.
>
> Verses 11-16 – The triumphant, conquering Christ appeared with His host of heaven.
>
> Verses 17-21 – The fowls of the air were called to devour the carnage from the conflict; the beast and the false prophet were thrown into the lake of fire.

Prayer Focus: Lord, what an exhilarating revelation that You are omnipotent and that You reign; help me to never forget it. Amen.
Notes:

Spiritual Journal:

Week: Fifty-two
Day: Wednesday
Book: Revelation
Chapter: Twenty
Memory Verse: Six
Principle: Everyone gets a chance at a fair and just trial before God Almighty.
Outline:

        Verses 1-3 – An angel binds Satan and casts him into the bottomless pit for a thousand years.

        Verses 4-6 – Following the first resurrection, the martyrs are established on thrones to rule during the coming thousand years.

        Verses 7-10 – At the end of the thousand years, Satan is loosed in order to give those who have never had the opportunity to make a decision for or against God a chance to rebel against Him. Following this brief period of deception, Satan is cast into the lake of fire.

        Verses 11-15 – At the conclusion of the thousand years, all the dead are resurrected and brought before the Great White Throne for final judgment and sentencing.

Prayer Focus: Lord, I ask You to judge me now and cover my sins with the blood of Christ so that I do not have to face Your ultimate judgment at the Great White Throne. Amen.
Notes:

Spiritual Journal:

Week: Fifty-two
Day: Thursday
Book: Revelation
Chapter: Twenty-one
Memory Verse: Four
Principle: The glory of heaven is not only in what it will contain (jewels, gold, and incredible beauty) and what will be missing (tears, sorrow, and death) but in Who will be there (the tabernacle of God will be with men and He will dwell with us).
Outline:
Verses 1-5 – At this point, everything is new: new heaven, new earth, New Jerusalem. All things are made new and all the former things, such as tears and sorrow, are passed away.
Verses 6-7 – Christ promises to freely give a full inheritance to the overcomers.
Verse 8 – The lake of fire is the inheritance promised to the sinner.
Verses 9-10 – One of the angels who brought the judgment upon the earth escorts John to see the bride of the Lamb, the New Jerusalem.
Verses 11-21 – The magnificent splendor of the city is described.
Verses 22-27 – The real glory of the city is the presence of the Lord and the redeemed saints who dwell there.
Prayer Focus: Lord, help me to inherit the kingdom You have prepared for me. Amen.
Notes:

Spiritual Journal:

Week: Fifty-two
Day: Friday
Book: Revelation
Chapter: Twenty-two
Memory Verse: Seven
Principle: Having painted a dramatic picture of the contrasting destinies of the righteous and the unrighteous (best case scenario versus worst case scenario), John closes the book with one final warning about another choice the reader can made that will affect which reward he will receive.

Outline:
Verses 1-5 – One final glimpse of the pleasantries of heaven is afforded.

Verses 6-7 – It is reaffirmed that Jesus, the faithful and true witness, is the one offering the opportunity to receive the blessing of heaven.

Verses 8-9 – A second time, John misplaces his worship.

Verses 10-15 – A command is given that the book not be sealed so that everyone will be aware of the coming of Christ and the pending reward or judgment.

Verses 16-20 – The validity of the book and its unalterable authority is verified by the testimonies of the angel, the Spirit, the bride, and Jesus Himself.

Verse 21 – The book concludes with a blessing.

Prayer Focus: Lord, as I conclude this year in Your Word, help me to make the right choices for my eternal destiny. Amen.

Notes:

Spiritual Journal:

Teach All Nations Mission

Teach All Nations Mission (TAN) is a global evangelical educational ministry birthed from the teaching ministries of Delron and Peggy Shirley. The name for Teach All Nations Mission was chosen to carefully indicate the exact heart of the Shirleys' mission. TAN's commitment is to establish a solid biblical foundation in national pastors and leaders so they can help enrich their own people. This vision is being accomplished by holding national leadership conferences and publishing and distributing Christian teaching materials in English and their local languages.

Someone accurately observed concerning the revival that is occurring in many parts of our world today that it is a mile wide but only an inch deep – the result of energetic evangelism by both missionaries and local Christians. Sadly, there is a marked shortage of teachers who are taking the next step in fulfilling our Lord's directive to teach them how to observe all that He has commanded. Therefore, Teach All Nations Mission has literally taken the words of Christ from Matthew 28:19, "Teach all nations," as its motto and mission statement.

TAN's commitment is to deepen that revival by training the pastors and leaders who then go back and strengthen their congregations. TAN pays for the travel and lodging of handpicked leaders because Delron and Peggy want to invest into their lives but know that these third-world saints could never afford to come at their own expense. TAN always provides the meals for all the guests during these conferences. The ministry also furnishes solid Christian literature in their local language or in English for those who understand the language.

Delron and Peggy realize that the challenge is much bigger than what they can accomplish in person; therefore, they have determined to expand the scope of their vision. One area of expansion includes a scholarship fund that will allow selected individuals to obtain a formal education in solid Christian colleges and Bible schools or through correspondence courses. The ministry has also assisted in building a Christian school in Zimbabwe and a Bible college in Nepal. Additionally, Teach All Nations assists the pastors and leaders they work with in times of need such as the tsunami in Sri Lanka, the earthquake in Nepal, and hurricanes in Belize and in the Turks and Caicos Islands. More recently, the ministry supported suffering Christians in twelve different nations who lost their source of income during the shutdowns during the COVID-19 pandemic.

Your gifts to and prayers for Teach All Nations will help the Shirleys continue their outreach to Christian leadership around the world.

Teach All Nations Mission
3210 Cathedral Spires
Colorado Springs, CO 80904
719-685-9999
www.teachallnationsmission.com
teachallnations@msn.com

Books by Delron & Peggy Shirley

Bingo, a Fresh Look at Grace
Christmas Thoughts
Cornerstones of Faith
Daily Bible Study Series (Five-Volume Set)
Daily Ditties from Delron's Desk
(Eight Volumes Available)
Doctor Livingstone, I Presume
Don't Leave Home Without It
Finally, My Brethren
Getting More UMPH out of Your Bible
Going Deeper in Jesus
The Great Commission – Doable
The IN Factors
In This Sign Conquer
Interface
Israel, Key to Human Destiny
The Last Enemy
Lessons Along the Way
Lessons from the Life of David
Living for the End Times
Maturing into the Full Stature of Jesus Christ
Maximum Impact
No Longer Bound
The Non-Conformer's Trilogy
Of Kings and Prophets
Passion for the Harvest
People Who Make A Difference
Positioned for Blessing and Power
Problem People of the Bible
Seeds and Harvest
The Seventh Man at the Well
So Send I You
So, You Wanna be a Preacher
Thirty-, Sixty-, One-Hundred-Fold
Tread Marks
Turning the World Upside Down and Back Again
Verse for the Day (Four Volumes Available)
Women for the Harvest
You'll be Darned to Heck
if You Don't Believe in Gosh
You Can Be Healed
Your Home Can Survive in the 21st Century
Your Part in the Grand Scheme of Things

Available at:
teachallnationsmission.com